RITE *of* PASSAGE
PARENTING
WORKBOOK

ABOUT THE AUTHORS

 WALKER MOORE, founder and president of Awe Star Ministries, is an internationally known youth culture expert, author, and conference speaker who has worked with families for more than three decades. His organization networks with thousands of churches worldwide to provide students with global missions opportunities.

Walker holds a Bachelor of Science and honorary Doctorate of Sacred Theology from Hannibal LaGrange College. Writing as a father who understands both the joys and heartaches of parenting, his humor and homespun wisdom touch hundreds of thousands of readers each week through his popular "Rite of Passage Parenting" column, featured in the *Baptist Messenger*.

Through Walker's practical teachings, families have rediscovered the joy of raising, not *children*, but capable, responsible, self-reliant *adults*. He speaks internationally to more than 150,000 people each year and is one of the primary speakers for Global Focus, a national, multidenominational service organization for church conferences. He and his wife, Cathy, have two adult sons.

 MARTI PIEPER finds great joy and fulfillment in helping translate Walker's teachings into print. She holds a Bachelor of Science from The Ohio State University and a Master of Divinity from Southwestern Baptist Theological Seminary. She has served as writer and editor for *Homeschooling Today* magazine and has assisted with several other book projects. She and her pastor husband, Tom, have five amazing children (three of whom have served internationally with Awe Star Ministries) who test and prove the *Rite of Passage Parenting* principles every day.

RITE *of* PASSAGE
PARENTING
WORKBOOK

Walker Moore
with Marti Pieper

THOMAS NELSON
Since 1798

NASHVILLE   DALLAS   MEXICO CITY   RIO DE JANEIRO   BEIJING

Published in Nashville, Tennessee, by Thomas Nelson. Thomas Nelson is a trademark of Thomas Nelson, Inc.

Thomas Nelson, Inc. titles may be purchased in bulk for educational, business, fundraising, or sales promotional use. For information, please e-mail SpecialMarkets@ThomasNelson.com.

Published in association with Yates & Yates, LLP, Attorneys and Counselors, Orange, California.

Scripture quotations, unless otherwise noted, are taken from *The Holy Bible*, The New King James Version®. © 1979, 1980, 1982, 1992 Thomas Nelson, Inc., Publishers.

Additional Scripture quotations are taken from the following sources:

(NIV) New International Version. © 1973, 1978, 1984, International Bible Society. Used by permission of Zondervan Bible Publishers.

(MSG) *The Message*, © 1993. Used by permission of NavPress Publishing Group.

(NCV) New Century Version®. © 1987, 1988, 1991 by Word Publishing, a Division of Thomas Nelson, Inc. Used by permission. All rights reserved.

(NASB) New American Standard Bible, © 1960, 1977 by the Lockman Foundation.

Rite of Passage Parenting Workbook

ISBN-10: 1-4185-1973-1
ISBN-13: 978-1-4185-1973-5

Printed in the United States of America
07 08 09 10 11 VIC 9 8 7 6 5 4 3 2 1

CONTENTS

INTRODUCTION

~

MAKE YOURSELF AT HOME

I'm so glad you bought this workbook. That tells me something important about you. It tells me . . . you're a good parent.

You see, you are much more than someone who bought a book—or two books, if you already own *Rite of Passage Parenting* (Nelson Books, 2007). (From now on, we'll use the acronym *ROPP*. That saves a lot of ink!) You may not have known it, but when you made that purchase and began to read my writing, you invited me into your home.

Just the other day, some friends of mine did the very same thing. They invited me over for dinner, and when I knocked on their door, they opened it wide. They seemed so glad to see me! I stepped inside the living room. The first thing I did was look around. I noticed the comfortable couch piled with pillows—the crowded bookshelves—the gilded antique clock commanding one corner of the room.

"Make yourself at home," my friends called back over their shoulders as they hurried out of the living room and down the hallway to the kitchen. "We're just putting the last few things together."

The unmistakable scents of cilantro, cumin, and chile powder drifted through the air as I sat waiting for my friends . . . and for the authentic Mexican meal I knew we were about to share. Tamales? Enchiladas? Something more exotic than I could pronounce? It didn't matter. It was going to be . . . food. My stomach growled, and I relaxed, my daydream leaving me certain that something delicious waited around the corner.

Meanwhile, back in the living room, I began to get a little impatient. "Make yourself at home," my friends had said. What did that really mean, anyway? As I began to ponder this thought, I noticed one or two books that, for some reason, stuck out several inches past the others on a nearby shelf. I jumped up to find a more suitable place for the misfits and then settled myself comfortably on the couch once more.

I'll be the first to admit it. I've logged way too many hours in front of HGTV—almost enough to be dangerous. In fact, my wife, Cathy, has pronounced me an *inferior* decorator. You can't blame a guy for trying, though. After I sat down, my eyes just happened to catch a painting that someone must have bumped. It tipped, very unevenly, to one side—right across from me on the western wall of the room. You guessed it. I jumped up from the couch, carefully adjusted the frame on its hanger, and sat back down again. I tried to ignore my stomach. By this time, it was growling even more urgently.

"Make yourself at home!" My hosts' thoughtful words echoed in my mind. "If this were really my home, I wouldn't have this chair here—I'd put it over there!" I thought, bouncing up from the couch one last time. "Let's see . . . I'd put this table over there, and that lamp definitely belongs on the other side of the room. Come to think of it—the couch would look much better if I just pulled it against that wall, and . . ." I was having so much fun moving furniture that I almost forgot my empty stomach.

Until my friends reappeared, that is. "Walker! What are you doing?" they said, as their eyes scanned the room and its altered decor. Somehow, their voices didn't sound quite as warm and welcoming as they had earlier.

"I was just . . . rearranging some furniture. You know . . . making myself at home!" I grinned, sure that my friends would understand and appreciate my good taste in interior design—or at least my sense of humor.

"Making yourself at home? Uh, Walker . . . we didn't really mean it."

Mom or Dad, I'm counting on the fact that, just like my fajita-serving friends, you'll let me make myself at home. Over the next few weeks, I plan to help you do some rearranging. You see, I believe you're such a good parent that you'll work with me to apply the principles I've learned through the years . . . right where your family needs them most. You want me to make myself at home, so you won't mind if I help you search out the areas that need changing. (If you've already read *ROPP*, you'll recognize that I want to expand, expound, open the window all the way up and help you . . . fix it, brother! Check out the Introduction to that book for the story of my unusual introduction to that phrase).

When I bring the ROPP principles into your family, I'll be the first to stand beside you and applaud your parenting. I'll even help you hang your successes on the wall for everyone to see! Since you're already a good parent, you'll tell me . . . "Make yourself at home." We may discover, though, that some of your furniture needs to be rearranged—maybe freshened up with a new slipcover or pillow. Finally, let's face it: we all have some junk or sour-smelling trash hiding in a closet or corner of our home. You and I will work together to carry those things out to the curb. We want to make sure that your family never stumbles over them again. When I help you do that, I know you'll tell me again to . . . "Make yourself at home."

As we spend the next few weeks going through ROPP together, you can expect to *laugh*. We'll spend time relaxing with this material and have fun as we grow together. Also, with the help this workbook provides, you will *learn* . . . just as I did when I began to study what was wrong with our culture and with today's kids. Most of all, you will receive encouragement designed to help you to *live*—to experience a new freedom in your parenting and family life.

You see, if you haven't already figured it out, ROPP is different from other parenting plans. Its distinctiveness begins with its goal. Instead of teaching you how to raise your children, I want to teach you to raise capable, responsible, self-reliant *adults*. As you learn to do that, you'll *live* by experiencing the kind of freedom that God has always intended for families to have.

I've designed this workbook to cover a six-week study period, although, of course, you can take longer to complete it if that works better for you or your group. Feel free to use it in the way that helps you the most. After all, you're a good parent—remember? You may choose to work through each session during a personal study, a time where you meet with your spouse, or a study group in which you meet with other good parents. If you're a Facilitator planning to use this workbook in a Bible study class, Sunday school, or other group meeting, I recommend that you read each session and answer the questions *before* your planned group time. In addition, group Facilitators, as well as those studying the material on their own, will want to check out the Facilitators' helps given in sidebars. Online support is also available at **www.ropparenting.com**. Here, you can download vidcasts (I call them ROPPcasts) of my teaching on ROPP, additional Facilitator's tips, and reproducible copies of Fix-It forms that allow you to customize the teachings and principles you'll come to understand through this text.

Children need the guidance, direction, and support of loving parents. This applies to workbooks and people alike! Since the *ROPP Workbook* has been designed to help you personalize the principles given in *ROPP*, you'll want to use the workbook alongside its parent book. I've listed the corresponding reading in *ROPP* at the beginning of each workbook session. Except for the first ("Make Yourself at Home") and Last ("Rite of Passage Parenting Celebration") sessions, each workbook session corresponds to an entire section (three chapters) of *ROPP*. If you've already finished *ROPP* and are just beginning the workbook, taking the time to look back over the chapters will help you get the most out of your study. To help refresh your memory, I've scattered helpful quotes from *ROPP* throughout the workbook.

ROPP: I love the scene [in the movie *Shrek*] in which Shrek and Donkey have reluctantly started on their way to save the princess. Donkey asks Shrek, "Who are you?" and Shrek explains that he is like an onion: He has many layers. (*Rite of Passage Parenting*)

Just like its parent book, the ROPP *Workbook* contains many layers. Check out the basic structure and features I'll use to make myself at home. Let's begin the process of reshaping your family and moving toward the goal of raising, not *children* but—capable, responsible, self-reliant adults.

USER'S GUIDE
SESSION FORMAT

MAKE YOURSELF AT HOME serves as the introduction to the study session, setting the scene for the work ahead. This section reviews both the ROPP Devotions from the previous week and the homework questions from the previous session. It will allow you a few minutes to get comfortable . . . as you prepare to have your family rearranged. (Suggested Group Time: 15–20 minutes)

WHAT'S MISSING? This section begins with some fun questions about the way things have changed in our society. You'll review one of the stories given in *ROPP*, and occasionally check out a new one. In addition, you'll start to think about the huge gaps that the agricultural-industrial shift has left in our culture and, more importantly, in our families. (Suggested Group Time: 10–15 minutes)

How It Shows: You'll begin this section by looking at statistics that show the dramatic effect that the cultural shift has had on families today. You will also examine a Bible teaching used in *ROPP*. You'll learn more about how the Bible applies specifically to the ways families raised young men and women before our country's shift from an agricultural to an industrial society. Through thought-provoking questions and discussion, this section will also help you begin to examine your own family and the ways the cultural shift hits home . . . in your home. (Suggested Group Time: 15–20 minutes)

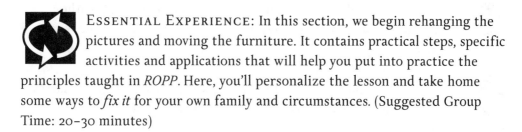 Essential Experience: In this section, we begin rehanging the pictures and moving the furniture. It contains practical steps, specific activities and applications that will help you put into practice the principles taught in *ROPP*. Here, you'll personalize the lesson and take home some ways to *fix it* for your own family and circumstances. (Suggested Group Time: 20–30 minutes)

ropp Devotionals: Five brief devotionals, designed to use at home on the weekdays following your completion of that session's study, will help you review and apply what you learn each week. Each one contains a **R**eading from God's Word, an **O**bservation in the form of a brief story, a **P**rinciple taken from *ROPP*, and a **P**rayer.

Session Features

Each session will also contain the following features:

 Facilitators: Instructions especially for those leading a study group, but also applicable to couples studying without a group or an individual studying alone. Make sure to check out the additional Facilitators' helps available at www.ropparenting.com.

ropp: Compelling quotes from this workbook's parent book, *Rite of Passage Parenting* (Nelson Books, 2007).

ʀᴏᴘᴘ Tᴇʀᴍꜱ: Callouts of special terms and definitions used in ʀᴏᴘᴘ.

 ʀᴏᴘᴘ Bʏ Tʜᴇ Nᴜᴍʙᴇʀꜱ: Lists of statistics closely tied to ʀᴏᴘᴘ, generally appearing in the "How It Shows" section.

 Cᴜʟᴛᴜʀᴇ Sʜᴏᴄᴋ: Real-life quotes that show the dramatic impact of the cultural shift on families today.

DᴀᴅSᴘᴇᴀᴋ: Specific suggestions for dads from a dad, *ROPP* author Walker Moore, husband of Cathy and father to Jeremiah and the infamous Caleb.

MᴏᴍSᴘᴇᴀᴋ: Mom-to-mom help from Walker's writing partner, Marti Pieper, whose four daughters and one son test and prove the ʀᴏᴘᴘ principles every day.

Wʜᴀᴛ Aʀᴇ ᴛʜᴇ Oᴅᴅꜱ? Testimonies from individuals whose lives have been shaped by the ʀᴏᴘᴘ principles.

51 Pᴇʀᴄᴇɴᴛ: Take-home assignments that provide practical, personal ways to implement truth . . . at least 51 percent of the time. Complete these between group sessions or between the weeks of your own individual study.

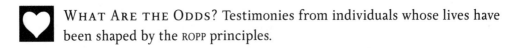 **Fɪx-Iᴛꜱ:** Example and template forms that provide specific ways to incorporate each of the four ʀᴏᴘᴘ essential experiences into your home. Use these to custom fit ʀᴏᴘᴘ to the specific needs of your family.

~

HANDLE WITH CARE

GOALS, SESSION ONE:

1. You will begin to understand and identify the roots of today's failure to produce capable, responsible, self-reliant adults: the rapid post-World War II shift from an agricultural to an industrial society.
2. You will begin to embrace the idea that you are a *good* parent who faces difficult challenges because of this cultural shift.
3. You will grow in your desire to learn and apply the "ancient path" of biblical principles of parenting to your own family life.

Welcome! Today marks a special day. You are reading these words because you are a *good* parent. I know you're a good parent because you cared enough to buy this *Rite of Passage Parenting Workbook*. Now, you can begin working through it on your own, with your spouse, or as a part of a study group. I want to welcome and encourage you: get ready! Get ready . . . for all the great things God intends to do in your

FACILITATORS: Before this session, please visit www.ropparenting.com and download the Session One ROPPcast. This vidcast contains the *How It Shows* Bible teaching with Walker Moore to use during the session. Similar ROPPcasts for each session are available on the site.

parenting and in your family life. He has wonderful plans for you and the ones you love.

If you've not already done so, I urge you to read the Introduction and User's Guide located immediately before this session. It explains the many *handles* you'll notice throughout these workbook pages. God intends you to grasp these handles tightly as you pick up ROPP and apply it to your own life. They will make it much easier for us when we start moving your family furniture around. The handles will help you understand the material more completely and give me a head start on . . . making myself at home.

⬤ ROPP: Without even thinking, my son said, "Dad, bad parents don't buy books." (*Rite of Passage Parenting*)

If you weren't already a *good* parent, you would never reach for handles in the first place. After all, only good parents think about things like improving their family life. You're the kind of good parent who's looking for handles that help you grasp God's Word, our world, and your family. You should know that the handles that jump out at you from the pages of the *ROPP Workbook* are the ones God intends to use very specifically in your life. They're the handles He intends for *you:* not your neighbor, and not the guy down the street. These handles may look a lot like the handles your parents used during your childhood—or they may be completely different. In fact, if you want to learn to *handle* your parenting even better than you already do . . . you've come to the right place.

I don't have all the answers—but I do have . . . handles. These have been shaped by years of study, prayer, and more than thirty years of working with young people and their families. They allow you to grab hold of the ROPP teachings and implement them in specific, practical ways. Today, we want to begin considering a huge handle that God showed me long ago: the cultural shift. Later, I'll explain more specifically what I mean, but for now . . . make yourself at home. In fact, sit on the couch—maybe even pop a bowl or two of popcorn. We're ready to watch a little TV!

MAKE YOURSELF AT HOME

Remember the 70s television show, *The Waltons*? Whether you watched it as a child, young adult, or only in today's cable reruns, almost everyone remembers John and Olivia Walton and their brood of seven active children. Just for a moment, fire up your imagination and recall some of those special slices of life on Walton's Mountain. Perhaps your mind will replay a scene at the long oak table in the kitchen, a day spent with John, Sr. and the boys out at the sawmill, or some moments spent rocking on the porch with Grandpa. Close your eyes and recall the sights, sounds, smells, tastes—even the feel of Walton's Mountain.

Welcome back! What was Walton's Mountain really like? Remember—you didn't just read about it—you were there! I want to start out with a challenge: Write down the names of as many of the Walton children as you can. If you're part of a group, work together and see if you can come up with all seven names as quickly as possible.

FACILITATORS: Use the first question set to initiate a fun discussion of life on Walton's Mountain as compared to today, introducing learners to the key concept that times have changed and our culture has shifted. If you want to add an extra-special touch, locate a DVD of a *Walton's* episode and play a few minutes here.

Now, think about your brief visit to Walton's Mountain and then about your own family's life today. Times really have changed. None of us can say that we live just as the Waltons did. Make a few notes about the differences you noticed in dress, speech, work, school, etc. between the Walton family and your own.

 FACILITATORS: The questions for this session often come in sets of two or three to provide learners an opportunity to examine the cultural shift by seeing how families have changed. Encourage group members to respond to each segment of a question set, if possible. For this set, share your own answers, and ask others to volunteer some of theirs. Consider posting these on a white board. As time allows, ask individuals to describe the items they chose for the time capsules and why. Make sure to affirm them for their participation and good memories.

WHAT'S MISSING?

Everyone likes nostalgia! We all enjoy looking to the past for expressions of meaning. In today's lesson, we will examine the ways our society has changed . . . and how that change affects families today.

Modern scientists have uncovered a time capsule that you, at age ten, buried in the backyard of your childhood home. List three elements it would be likely to contain (for example, an eight-track tape, a banana seat from your favorite bike, and a stuffed Care Bear).

1.

2.

3.

Think about your parents or grandparents. Answer the above question as if they had buried the time capsule as children. Even if you cannot name three items, try to list at least one or two.

1.

2.

3.

Now for the real challenge: can you name the items your child (children) would include in a time capsule made today? If you do not have children yet, answer the question for a child you know well.

1.

2.

3.

HOW IT SHOWS

My own journey toward ROPP began when, as a youth minister, I confronted a huge problem more than thirty years ago.

CULTURE SHOCK: *Even at ten years old, while growing up in a suburb north of Boston, Jessica F. was in and out of trouble. She had tried drinking and smoking, and had developed a habit of constantly lying to her parents. When it came time for her to get her driver's license, Jessica's parents were scared to death. . . . So, her stepfather Mark Pawlick bought what's called a black box and hid it in Jessica's car. By using global positioning system technology (GPS) to fix its location every second or so, the device is essentially an electronic tattletale. It automatically e-mails or calls Pawlick every time Jessica drives too fast, or goes somewhere she isn't supposed to. More and more teens will have to get used to the idea of "Big Mother" looking over kids' shoulders. With GPS technology getting cheaper, smaller and better, most any cell phone can be a tracking device for just a few extra dollars a month. A black box, like the one made by Alltrack that's in Jessica's car, costs a few hundred dollars, plus a monthly fee . . . Many experts believe such tracking devices will soon be as mainstream as cell phones themselves.*

"I think, over time, parents will feel if they don't have this, they're not being good parents," says Jim

 ROPP: No matter how much Bible teaching I did, no matter how many activities I planned, no matter how much I prayed and spent time with the students, I did not see real growth in their lives. Nearly all of them were still dealing with exactly the same problems as seniors in high school that they faced in their early teens. In fact, they took these struggles along to college, on to their jobs, and into their marriages. Very few of them ended up as responsible, capable adults. Why was my work so ineffective? Why weren't the students maturing as God intended? I didn't know what to do. I began to label myself a failure, and I was ready to quit youth ministry altogether. Their parents and I had the same question: "What's wrong with our kids, anyway?" *(Rite of Passage Parenting)*

Katz, Director of the Rutgers University Center for Mobile Communication Studies.[1]

There's no doubt about it. You had a response to this "Culture Shock" story as soon as you finished reading it. Circle the letter of the comment below that most closely resembles your thoughts:

> *a. Wow! This guy is being so careful—he must be a really good parent.*
> *b. Oh no! I don't think the daughter should drive anything more powerful than a bike.*
> *c. Oooh. This dad has a real problem—and I'm not sure it's just his daughter.*
> *d. Cool! Where can I get the number for the black box company?*

No one would argue against the idea that our society has changed drastically since World War II, but do we recognize the impact of those changes on families today? Play the following High-Low Game as you continue thinking about the cultural shift.

Listed below are some statistics about American family life today. Mark each with an **H** ("Higher") or **L** ("Lower"), indicating whether you believe the actual number is higher or lower than the one given here.

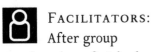 **FACILITATORS:** After group members have finished marking the ROPP BY THE NUMBERS list, form two teams (men versus women or another grouping). Ask team members to share answers and reach a consensus for each question. Have fun exchanging ideas as you proceed through the list of statistics. You may be surprised by how much—or how little—your group knows about our culture!

 ROPP BY THE NUMBERS:

1. 55 . . . percent of twenty-somethings today who attended church as teens are not now actively praying, reading the Bible, or attending church.

2. 47 . . . percent of grandparents whose relationship

with their grandchildren, geographically and/or emotionally, is best described as "remote."

3. 30 . . . percent of last year's college graduates still live with their parents (2006 statistics).

4. 28 . . . percent of 18- to 20-year olds have parents who help them with chores.

Now, think about your own family. Since we're talking about numbers, I'm picking one of my favorites: twenty-one. I want you to keep this number in mind when you consider our next set of questions.

Where did you live and what was your job/school when you were twenty-one years old?

What about your dad (if you're a dad) or mom (if you're a mom)? Answer the same questions for him (her) at age twenty-one.

FACILITATORS: If you are working with a group, you will need to allow more time for discussion at this point. By now, God's Holy Spirit will have begun the process of binding group members' hearts together, and the cultural shift will begin to naturally reveal itself as the answers unfold. Those who have offspring as old as twenty-one may choose to answer from their own parenting experience, but avoid pressuring anyone to share responses.

Actual Answers:

1. (actual answer, 61%)[2]

2. (actual answer, 29)[3]

3. (actual answer, 44%)[4]

4. (actual answer, 57%, averaging out to 527 hours a year)[5]

Finally, think all the way back to your grandparents. Again—men, think of your grandfather, and women, think of your grandmother, and answer those same questions once more! (If you don't know, and your grandparents are still living, this would make a great reason to ask them.)

MomSpeak: *At first, the whole idea of a cultural shift did nothing but overwhelm me. What could something that sounded so big and confusing have to do with the way Tom and I raised our kids? When I began to think closer to home (read "like a mom"), this concept became much more real.*

I looked at my dad's life. He grew up on a farm during the Depression/World War II era. By the time he was raising his own kids during the 1960s and 1970s, he had graduated from college with an engineering degree, begun working for a large corporation, and moved our family to a bedroom community of Cincinnati. Things had changed a lot since

Dad was a boy! After all, he was driving tractors and doing a man's work in the fields when he was still in elementary school. No wonder the comfortable suburban neighborhood where we lived or the ways my brother and I spent our time made very little sense to him.

Think about your own family through the generations. You don't have to look far to realize that the changing culture has reshaped the way we live. Where did your parents grow up? Their parents? When you look at it from this more personal angle, I think you'll start to see how the cultural shift affects you and your family every day.

The Bible teaches us that we should not only *look* to the past in nostalgia, but also that we should *learn* from its wise instruction. Jeremiah tells us, "**Thus says the LORD, 'Stand by the ways and see and ask for the ancient paths, Where the good way is, and walk in it; And you will find rest for your souls'**" (Jeremiah 6:16 NASB).

Nearly every day, I deal with people who do not have rest for their souls. They're doing the best they can—but their families are broken. They've tried to do everything right—but their kids have turned out wrong. I faced these same struggles during my years of youth ministry. In fact, these struggles started me on the journey that brought me to the principles of ROPP. I wanted to find out how to "fix it" for the hopeless, helpless, hurting parents and young people I worked with every day. I wanted to show them how to find peace, satisfaction, and . . . rest.

Since the Scriptures told me that *rest* came from returning to the "ancient paths," I began to wonder: Exactly what are these paths? As I studied this passage, I looked at the word *ancient,* or in Hebrew, *olam.* I discovered that *olam* does not mean chronologically

FACILITATORS: Play the Bible teaching segment of the Session One ROPPcast at this time. If you choose not to use this option, make sure to go over the Bible teaching in the next few paragraphs and prepare to explain or read alongside your group and/or partner.

old, but *concealed, original, timeless, out of eternity.* That meant that an "ancient path" is a path from eternity past to eternity future.

Think back with me to the beginning—the very beginning of life in Genesis 1. When God created the heavens and earth and everything in them, He pronounced His creation *good* in every way. He not only stamped "goodness" *upon* them, but He also embedded it *within* them, implanting it within the core of their being. Each of the many elements of His amazing creation was built for eternity, timeless, with its own intentional design and purpose that was *good.*

Have you ever watched as a flock of geese flies south for the winter? Have you seen a retriever lift its nose and tail as it "points" toward a bird? Every summer and fall, hundreds of squirrels visit my backyard, filling their cheeks with nuts that they bury and put away for colder days. No one taught these animals to carry out these tasks. I began to realize that these unconscious, purposeful behaviors—the ones scientists call *instinct*—are the *ancient paths* that God implanted within His creation.

Every single animal, every plant and tree, every star and planet—every part of His creation has His ancient paths built deep inside it. Man can certainly manipulate the ancient path. He can train the dog or cause the hatchling goose to imprint to himself rather than to another goose—but he cannot change the Creator's hidden intention. God has built His ancient order into His creation, and each component lives out the design He has implanted within it.

As a unique part of God's creation, man also has "ancient paths" deep within His design. He is the only aspect of creation that God described with the superlative—He pronounced man "*very* good."

However, man is also the one element of God's creation that has a will, allowing him to accept or reject His way. We follow God's ancient paths for our lives not by *instinct,* but by *obedience*—by choice.

Deep within our hearts, God has placed the design for life. He has concealed inside us the desire and ability to build wholesome, healthy families that produce capable, responsible, self-reliant adults who will build wholesome, healthy families and . . . you get the picture. God has this wonderful design stamped on the very fiber of our being! When we willfully reject it by turning away from Him, we go out on our own paths and reject His eternal purposes for our lives.

As I went on my journey to discover how to "fix it" for my family and others, I noticed that other cultures contained some experiences that ours lacked. I could go deep into the jungles of Panama with the Embera Puru people, or into the heart of the Karamajong tribe in Uganda, and find the same essential experiences. These people did not struggle to produce capable, responsible, self-reliant adults. In fact, their children crossed the line from childhood to adulthood naturally, appropriately, and at much younger ages than those in our advanced Western world. I began to wonder if the solution to what's missing in our parenting lay in these ancient paths that the other cultures retained.

Jeremiah tells us that when we're in trouble, when things are not going well, it's time to stop and evaluate. He encourages us to "see" and "ask," to survey our lives and see whether we are raising our children according to the ancient paths, according to the good way in which God designed for us to live.

The Enemy of our souls has a problem with that. Since he knows that the ancient paths placed within

ROPP: While I was struggling with the problems in the lives of these students, I began to study teenage culture, and I discovered something amazing. Our society's downward plunge accelerated during the post-World War II era, when we completed the move from an agricultural to an industrial society. Young married couples moved farther away from their parents, following the lure of large companies and secure employment. People left the farms and moved closer to their jobs and schools for their children.

As a result, we made a very rapid switch from a day where the generations lived and worked together to one in which the family unit became much more isolated. . . . Neither my generation nor the ones following it have done any better than their parents at producing capable kids. The "expert" advice on which parents depended

our hearts will bring us closer to God and His truth, he tries any tricks he can to lead families away from it. No, the devil doesn't make us do it—but he certainly mixes up our culture and whispers lies to us about what we should and shouldn't do as parents. The resulting cultural chaos has robbed families of the ability to raise capable, responsible, self-reliant children by taking them far away from the will and Word of God.

As you read *ROPP* and begin to apply its principles through this workbook, I'm praying you'll find it pointing you not to me, but to the ancient paths that God has placed within you. When you do, you will find a new joy in parenting. Then you will find "rest for your souls."

 ## ESSENTIAL EXPERIENCE: RITE OF PASSAGE PARENTING

WHAT ARE THE ODDS? I have lived and worked in lower Alabama off and on for over fifty years. As a boy, I experienced the thrill of riding with my family out to the cotton-white fields on a wagon full of equally poor folks. We were all just trying to survive.

We would work all day sunup to sundown, dragging eight-foot cotton sacks down the rows of cotton, picking it from the sharp husks, pushing it into the sacks. What did we get for our efforts? Five cents a pound, bleeding fingers, sore backs—and something much more valuable. At Saturday morning paydays, adults pooled their money with their children, buying just the basics: fatback to add to the beans, a chicken, a new pair of shoes, even some clothes. Life was tough, but we learned that the family who pulled together would have its needs met—some of them, anyway. Even as children, we did an adult's work, and we took pride in our accomplishments. We knew that we mattered.

After thirty years in the U.S. Army and about twenty years in the mental health field as a Licensed Professional Counselor and the CEO of my own counseling business, I see a vastly different population of people with, for the most part, far different values and standards. No longer do families work in the fields to bring in the crop of cotton and (now) peanuts here in the Wiregrass. Instead, large machines and tractors take mere hours to pick a field clean. Fathers ride in the air-conditioned cabs of their monster machines while their kids sit at home playing XBox or Game Boy, or watching the latest twisted production on their widescreen TVs. The violence that surrounds them has desensitized many of them to the devaluation of life that has now become commonplace. Crack, pot, and crystal meth dealers can be found anywhere, anytime, adding to the downward spiral of young lives with no purpose or cause, no self-respect, no concern for the dignity or safety of others.

No doubt about it: Our young people today are faced with an outpouring of vile stimuli . . . In my counseling business, I am seeing more and more children who are the product of a generation of people who have no direction, structure, or purpose in their own lives and are unable to provide for their offspring what they don't have themselves.

ROPP provides parents with the tools to raise children to become capable, responsible, self-reliant adults. I have seen these materials work over and over again in my private counseling practice. I truly

did not stop the cultural shift or its dramatic, devastating impact. The downward plunge that began in the 1950s has not yet stopped. Even with all our progress, even with the advent of color TVs, CDs, DVDs and MP3s and all the other high-priced, high-tech gadgets that we consider so essential today, we can't seem to raise kids who are normal—kids who grow up into capable, responsible, self-reliant adults. It's time someone cried out, "Enough is enough!" or even, "Fix it, brother!"

FACILITATORS: To make the next group discussion more comfortable, allow members to answer both questions and then discuss as one unit ("Let's talk about the ways you were disciplined and the ways you discipline") without posting answers on a board. Some people will feel more comfortable than others in discussing this topic, especially at this early point. If time allows, you can use this question set as a bridge into a discussion of other ways we do things differently than our parents, and why this might be true.

believe that they will prepare families to stand against the destructive values and standards of our world today.[6]

—*John David Rook, MS, LPC, NCC*
Counseling of the Wiregrass, LLC (Counseling Plus)
258 South Paint Avenue
Ozark, AL 36360

Do you get the message? Times have changed! The culture has shifted. Has our parenting shifted along with it? Let's examine that in the next two question sets.

The word **discipline** *means correction with intent to teach or train. Think back to the way your parents corrected and taught you (and your siblings, if any) as a child. List some of the specific ways they did this. Examples include loss of privilege, physical punishment (spanking), verbal rebuke, etc.*

Now, think about the ways you discipline your own children. List them here. Write an **S** *or* **D** *next to each one to indicate whether you believe it to be* **S***imilar to or* **D***ifferent than the ways you received instruction, correction, and training as a child.*

 DADSPEAK: Discipline? *What about good old-fashioned* punishment? *Maybe I can explain.*

I grew up on the principle, "Spare the rod and spoil the child." In fact, I can't think of many times when Dad spared the rod from any of us boys.

During my own early years as a father, I noticed that I actually enjoyed spanking my sons. I'm like most guys. I don't want to talk about the problem—I want to "fix it, brother." Spanking seemed like a good means to . . . an end.

I soon figured out that I wasn't fixing things nearly as well as I thought. Sure, spanking my sons always made me feel better—after all, I had taken action to address an obvious need. What didn't seem quite right was my boys' behavior after the spankings. It didn't change much at all. What's more, as I began to study the Scriptures, I noticed Ephesians 6:4: "Fathers, do not make your children angry, but raise them with the training and teaching of the Lord" (NCV). How did this apply to spanking?

FACILITATORS: Since you want to end your group session in a way that encourages members to return, make sure to allow for this closing time even if you have to eliminate something else. After participants answer the following question, invite them to share their responses with the person beside them. After each one finishes, his or her listener will say, in a very affirming tone, "Wow! You are a good parent! I admire you because you (*name the specific behavior that shows what a good parent he or she is*)."

Once this is finished, read the ROPP Contract together and have each individual sign his or her own page. After that, members should sign one another's books as a mark of surrender and accountability. If possible, close in a time of prayer for all the good parents who intend to become even better ones.

Couples studying this

I happen to believe that in certain cases, especially with young children, spanking can be done the right way. I also know that very often, the right way just doesn't happen. When a spanking crosses the line from discipline to punishment, it not only makes children angry, it's . . . wrong.

Discipline ("the training and teaching of the Lord") does not provoke your child to anger. Instead, it instills values and corrects character faults.

Punishment (whether through a spanking or some other means) satisfies the needs of the parent. Discipline, on the other hand, meets the needs of the child.

Dad (mom, too): parenting is like many other things in life. You can pay now, or pay later. We must rediscover the ancient path of expending time, energy, and effort to discipline our children instead of *punishing* them. *This path costs a great deal. Are the results worth the price?*

Are your children?

I hope this session has helped you begin to think about the dramatic cultural shift that has affected families in so many ways. I also hope you come away realizing that you are a *good* parent. You're looking for answers in just the right places: God's Word, this workbook, and your study group, if you're a part of one.

Let's finish today by reminding one another who we are. In this space, write a few words that describe something you know about the person to your right, maybe even something spoken tonight, that shows . . . he or she is a good parent. Maybe he mentioned leaving work early to attend the group meeting. Maybe she spoke about her concern for a troubled child, of how she wants to learn even one thing that will help her become an even better parent—what was it? Write it down here. After you share your responses as instructed, turn to the ROPP Contract, FIX-IT #1-1, page 25.

% 51 PERCENT: I like to tell parents that I don't expect perfection . . . from them or from their kids. I know you won't apply the ROPP principles twenty-four hours a day, seven days a week. After all, I didn't even do that when my sons were growing up! Instead, I know that you are already good parents, the kind who will become even better if you apply these ROPP principles . . . just fifty-one percent of the time. That's because if you practice ROPP *more often than not*, you'll be way ahead of the culture—you'll *handle* your parenting much more responsibly than most parents today.

That's also why I'm choosing to call the homework for this workbook *51 Percent.* I know you will care enough to take time to complete these 51 Percent tasks between group sessions or individual studies, because . . . you are a *good parent.*

This week, concentrate on the following ROPP handles:

1. Use the space below to write a brief summary of a media message you notice this week that illustrates the cultural shift (Example: a television news feature about parents who write term papers for their college-age children; a magazine article about how families have changed since World War II).

material without a group should take the time to affirm one another and sign the contract together. Good parents who study the material alone will also want to take the time to sign the contract, partnering with God and realizing how honored He is with your commitment and perseverance. Even if you're working alone, don't skip the time of affirmation; instead, ask your heavenly Father to show you one thing that causes Him to say to you: *you are a good parent.*

2. Write one or two sentences here about something you do this week that reminds you once again: You are a *good* parent. Perhaps you played basketball with your son when you would have preferred to watch the news. Maybe you affirmed your daughter for the hard work she did on that school project. If you are part of a study group, be prepared to report on this good news at your next session.

3. If you have the opportunity, read and/or review "Essential Experience #1: Rite of Passage," chapters 1–3 in *Rite of Passage Parenting*.

4. Over a five-day period before beginning the next lesson, read and study this chapter's ROPP Devotion Guide beginning just after Fix-It #1–1. Next, complete the following: *Sometimes, God speaks to us through others' insights. Which of this week's devotional readings seemed to contain His personal note to you? Why? Write its title here, along with a few words that remind you what God said and how you responded.*

FIX-IT #1-1
RITE OF PASSAGE PARENTING CONTRACT

Thus says the Lord, "Stand by the ways and see and ask for the ancient paths,
Where the good way is, and walk in it; And you will find rest for your souls"
(Jeremiah 6:16 NASB).

I AM A GOOD PARENT. I care about my children, and I want to help them face the challenges of our changing culture. I know I can become an even better parent by returning to the "ancient paths" that God has designed and instilled within me as a beloved part of His creation.

THEREFORE, believing that God has created me with both the deep desire and ability to become a Rite of Passage Parent, I purpose in my heart to participate in this study. I surrender my time to prayerfully studying the materials and completing homework assignments each week. In this way, I will be a capable, responsible, self-reliant student who will hold other good parents accountable for completing their work, expecting them to do the same for me.

(signed) _____ (participant)

_____

_____

_____

_____

_____

RITE OF PASSAGE PARENTING DEVOTION GUIDE

DAY ONE: DUMB AND DUMBER

READING: *His lord said to him, "Well done, good and faithful servant; you were faithful over a few things, I will make you ruler over many things. Enter into the joy of your lord"* (Matthew 25:21).

OBSERVATION: Do you ever wonder why people do the things they do?

Every year, I enjoy reading about the recipients of the Darwin Awards. These honors "salute the improvement of the human genome by honoring those who accidentally remove themselves from it."[7] Newspaper articles describing the fatal deeds ultimately lead to Web site nominations and honors.

Some nominees:

- A man in Alabama who died from a rattlesnake bite. He and a friend decided to amuse themselves by playing catch, not with a ball or a Frisbee, but with a rattlesnake. In the process, both men were bitten. One died, and the other was hospitalized. The article failed to explain exactly what might motivate two grown men to play catch with a snake.
- A twenty-year-old from Wesley Chapel, Florida, who was hit in the leg with pieces of the bullet he fired at the exhaust pipe of his car. As he repaired the car, he realized that he needed to bore a hole in this pipe. Failing to find a drill, he tried to shoot a hole in it instead.
- A drunken security guard working at a bank in Moscow who asked a colleague to stab his bulletproof vest to see if it would protect him against a knife attack. It did not, and this twenty-five-year-old died of a heart wound.
- A thirty-four-year-old man from Alamo, Michigan, who was killed in March as he was trying to repair what police described as a "farm-type truck." This man got a friend to drive the truck down a highway while he hung underneath to ascertain the source of a troubling noise. His clothes caught on something, however, and the other man found him "wrapped in the drive shaft."

After reading about these awards, I feel better about myself as a parent. My boys have made some big mistakes, but they have not done anything that would earn them a Darwin Award. They don't always make the right choices. Sometimes they do things that get on my nerves. Still, I realize that they, like their dad, are a work in progress.

Relax, take a break, and enjoy your children. If someone asks you how your kids are doing, just say "Great! We have made it another year without being nominated for . . . the Darwin Awards."

PRINCIPLE: You are a much better parent than you think.

PRAYER: *Dear Father, Satan wants to convince me that I am a bad parent. Help me come against the confusion, frustration, and depression that cause me to focus on the negative. With Your wisdom, I will improve my parenting. Help me to continue to work hard at nurturing my children. Today, I praise You for Your grace, and thank You for showing me the good things I do. Amen.*

DAY TWO: OUR NATIONAL MONUMENT

READING: *For this reason I bow my knees to the Father of our Lord Jesus Christ, from whom the whole family in heaven and earth is named, that He would grant you, according to the riches of His glory, to be strengthened with might through His Spirit in the inner man* (Ephesians 3:14–16).

OBSERVATION: We had just bought our first house and needed to furnish it. The first item on our shopping list? A refrigerator. We hoped to find something on sale. The clerk took us straight to the fancy models—the kind that do everything except change diapers. I was very impressed, but I explained our situation and let the salesman know that we were looking for something a little less upscale.

Mentally watching his commission plummet, our guide took us to the lower end of the refrigerator food chain. Even these cost more than we could afford. I politely asked if the store ever sold used appliances. Rolling his eyes in disgust, the salesman told us about a slightly damaged model. He could offer it to us at a substantial reduction if we would take it "as is."

There it stood: A beautiful gold-toned, eighteen-cubic-foot beauty, seemingly dropped out of heaven just for us. The "slight" damage was a good-sized dent on the left side. I knew I could hide the defect against the kitchen counter, and the price was certainly right.

That refrigerator remained a beloved member of the Moore family for eighteen years. Eventually, it began to struggle. I heard it wheezing as it strained to keep our food and beverages cool. Although it never complained, I knew its days were numbered. One afternoon, it just quit.

When I called the 911-appliance hotline, the specialist merely patted me on the back and told me to let it go. He saw . . . an old dented refrigerator. I saw . . . a national monument to the lives of our family members. It proudly displayed our sons' very first artwork. It also held pictures, report cards, sports awards, doctor's appointment reminders, and newspaper clippings.

As our boys matured and our lives got even busier, the refrigerator held school calendars, notes to one another, and even college class schedules. If it was significant to our family, you found it—there on the refrigerator.

Today, our monument has been replaced with a new, white, high-tech, side-by-side model with ice and water dispenser and without a single dent. It does the job . . . but it has no character.

Family is important. Our old refrigerator, holding everything from baby bottles to corsages for our sons' prom dates, reminded me of that daily. Now, it sits, silent and lonely, in our garage. I still hold out a faint hope that the Smithsonian will call me, asking to display . . . our national monument.

PRINCIPLE: We must treasure our families as a gift from God.

PRAYER: *Dear Father, Just calling You "Father" reminds me that I am part of a much bigger family. Keep reminding me of the importance of my earthly family, and help me make them my daily priority. Amen.*

DAY THREE: COMPUTER CURSE

READING: *Blessed are the undefiled in the way, Who walk in the law of the LORD! Blessed are those who keep His testimonies, Who seek Him with the whole heart! They also do no iniquity; They walk in His ways. You have commanded us To keep Your precepts diligently* (Psalm 119:1–4).

OBSERVATION: Computers: you can't live with them, and . . . they don't make very good paperweights. I was born a generation too early to have a hope of becoming truly computer literate. If computers are supposed to be timesavers that reduce paper use, then why does it now take me twice as long to get things done, and why do I still have piles of paper cluttering my office?

When you own a computer, not only do you have to learn an entirely new language, but sooner or later, you must deal with a paper jam. Have you ever tried to pull a piece of paper from a computer printer? It should qualify as an Olympic sport. First, you straddle the printer, planting one foot firmly on each side. Putting a death grip on the leading edge, you pull the paper with hurricane force . . . and it doesn't budge. You rip it out in one mighty jerk, leaving an ungraspable portion stuck between the roller bars. Finally, you are reduced to removing the remainder . . . one sliver at a time.

I call my computer *Cyclops.* It has a single eye in the middle of its forehead, and we spend the day staring each other down. Computers, like dogs and horses, can sense fear in human beings. Mine believes I will back down at the least little "error" notice, so I approach it with care. My confidence comes only from knowing that at any time, I can pull its plug and render the beast helpless.

In today's fast-paced world, we look for the newest, quickest ways to deal with problems . . . even in parenting. Every bookstore holds a plethora of self-help books, all promising the latest and greatest way to deal with your children. In our search, we tend to ignore the greatest parenting book ever written: *the Bible.* It contains timeless truths, relevant advice, and a real guarantee. ROPP tries to teach parents to return to the "ancient paths" (Jeremiah 6:16) of Scripture. That makes this workbook, not a self-help book, but a "God, help!" book.

You'll be glad to know that I have now conquered my computer problems. If it doesn't do what I say . . . I threaten to turn it over to a child!

PRINCIPLE: Don't ignore the number-one source of parenting advice: the Bible.

PRAYER: *Lord, thank You for the answers You give us in Your Word. Thank You that You care about our children even more than we do, and that You will teach us how to become the parents they need. Amen.*

DAY FOUR: CHOICES AND CHANGES

READING: *Bow down Your ear to me. Deliver me speedily; Be my rock of refuge, A fortress of defense to save me. For You are my rock and my fortress; Therefore, for Your name's sake, Lead me and guide me. Pull me out of the net which they have secretly laid for me, For You are my strength* (Psalm 31:2–4).

OBSERVATION: Every time I return from the mission field, I find myself dealing with reverse culture shock. Even when I leave the country for just a short time, I come home to find that things have changed. It seems as though I am always in the process of having to relearn how to live in America. A few years ago, when I returned home after an extended trip, I learned something that really upset me. I could not believe our country had sunk so low as to trifle with the most sacred aspects of life. While I was away, Heinz announced that they were going to begin producing green ketchup.

Green ketchup? I just knew this was going against the natural order of the universe. Mustard is yellow. Green beans are . . . green. And ketchup is *red*! It has always been red. Adam and Eve had red ketchup. George Washington had red ketchup. My parents had red ketchup. Only a demented corporate executive could have decided that suddenly, ketchup should be green.

In a changing world, home should provide continuity and stability. These two essentials enable a child to feel secure in an ever-changing world. Kids have the daily challenge of figuring out how to fit in with our culture's constant adjustments to "acceptable" and "not acceptable." Our world is changing faster than at any point in the history of mankind. Technology makes even today's world obsolete . . . tomorrow.

A society filled with contradictions magnifies the importance of the home. If your home does not provide a sanctuary from the world, then your child is surrounded by confusion and chaos. Instead, home should be a place of constant acceptance, love, and encouragement.

When I come back from overseas, I want to go . . . home. Besides, I know I'll find red ketchup waiting there. Heinz wisely took the green kind off the market.

PRINCIPLE: Even in a world of changes, a child feels secure when there is stability in the home.

PRAYER: *Dear Father, You are my Rock! In an ever-changing world, You are the same yesterday, today and tomorrow. May You be the Rock of this home and the Rock of my children. When the ill winds of culture try to blow them away, may their roots run deep in You, and may they find sanctuary and stability in our home. Amen.*

DAY FIVE: CIRCUS PONY

READING: *"And these words which I command you today shall be in your heart. You shall teach them diligently to your children, and shall talk of them when you sit in your* *house, when you walk by the way, when you lie down, and when you rise up. You shall bind them as a sign on your hand, and they shall be as frontlets between your eyes. You shall write them on the doorposts of your house and on your gates"* (Deuteronomy 6:6–9).

OBSERVATION: My wife grew up outside the city limits of Hannibal, Missouri—the home of Mark Twain. Like every other child, Cathy longed for a horse. Her family had the land for it. But owning a horse was a luxury . . . and only rich folks had luxuries.

One day, a man from the city asked about renting a pasture where he could keep a horse. Cathy's dad realized he could earn money and provide a way for his little girl to ride.

The man agreed, and the horse was delivered. You can imagine Cathy's excitement! She envisioned herself riding at full gallop, trim little body bouncing in the saddle, long, blonde hair flowing behind.

Unfortunately, the boarding animal turned out to be not a horse, but a diminutive Shetland pony with an unusual habit. It had spent most of its life traveling with those kiddy circuses that set up in parking lots, harnessing several ponies to an awkward contraption that resembles a treadmill.

The only life this pony knew was walking in tiny circles, little children straddling its back. Whenever Cathy tried to ride, the pony just walked around and around. There was no long gallop, no flowing hair—only plodding in a circle, day after day, ride after ride.

This story happens in too many families. We have glorious dreams of marriage and child-rearing, but before long, our lives become a parking lot sideshow. We end up walking in circles of silence around the treadmill of hopelessness.

The enemy longs to turn our families into parking lot pony rides, and we settle for his tricks. When Jesus said that He came to give us life abundantly (John 10:10), He also meant families. God created families to display His love and joy. He intended our homes to become a tiny glimpse of heaven this side of eternity.

We tend to treat each other the way our parents treated each other, raise our children the way we were raised, and handle problems the way our parents handled problems. Instead, we need to bring our families under new management. When we yield our minds and hearts to Him, we will no longer go in circles. Remember: the one whom Jesus sets free is . . . free indeed.

PRINCIPLE: Don't just raise your kids the way you were raised, but yield to God's pattern and plan for the family.

PRAYER: *Lord, help me teach my children about You every day. Keep my family from becoming a sideshow, and let us look to You to set us free. Amen.*

RITE OF PASSAGE

GOALS, SESSION TWO:

1. You will begin to understand and identify the need to provide your child/children with a *rite of passage, a clearly defined line that distinguishes childhood from adulthood.*
2. You will begin to embrace the idea that, as good parents who seek the "ancient paths," you want to provide a rite of passage for your child/children.
3. You will begin to develop practical ways to institute rite of passage (including rite of passage preparation, event, and celebration) in your own home and family.

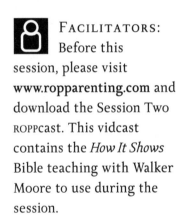 MAKE YOURSELF AT HOME

I'm glad to see you again! As we make ourselves at home in the workbook and in your family once more, let's begin with a quick look at what God has done during the past week.

In *ROPP* and in my teaching ministry, I tell a lot of stories. In fact, I tell a lot of stories about my two

FACILITATORS: Before this session, please visit **www.ropparenting.com** and download the Session Two ROPPcast. This vidcast contains the *How It Shows* Bible teaching with Walker Moore to use during the session.

FACILITATORS:
As the group gathers, encourage members to begin sharing their responses to the 51 Percent assignments from Session One (page 23). At some point, make sure to stop and pray for your time together. Consider asking a member who would be comfortable doing so to open in prayer for all the good parents present.

sons—especially Caleb, the one I call my *special* child. Through the years, our youngest son's creative approach to life has often managed to surprise his mother and me. Even today, whenever we think we've seen it all, he manages to amaze us one more time.

One of my favorite stories about Caleb appears in ROPP. On parent-teacher conference night, the nurse at his middle school anxiously approached us as we walked down the hall. It seemed that she was very concerned about our son's low blood sugar episodes, which were becoming more and more frequent. When Caleb felt one of them coming on, he headed to her office to rest on a cot and eat one of the candy bars she kept especially for him. His mother and I saw just one small problem with that scenario: Caleb didn't have diabetes—just a creative mind and a not-so-holy hunger for candy bars.

Caleb's approach to life always contrasts with the organized, efficient one of his older brother, Jeremiah. When he graduated from high school, Jeremiah handed me a gift: a typed, single-spaced list of his most important values. The list went on and on . . . and on. It contained not five, not ten, but more than two hundred pages in all!

I love my boys. As different as they are, their lives reflect the ancient paths that God has instilled within them. They also reflect something I tell parents nearly every day: *there's no such thing as a normal child.*

You may not have a child who fakes diabetes to earn free candy bars, or even one who types out a list of his most important values, but most parents seem to agree: in today's world, there's "no such thing as a normal child." Write a few words on the following page to summarize one of your own stories about one or more of your children—something amusing, interesting or just plain goofy that he or she did or said. If you're part of a group, prepare to share with your friends.

FACILITATORS:
Plan to cover one or more of the following questions as a group. When members share, respond with affirming words. Remember: The ROPP goals extend beyond right answers. We are working together to help parents interact with these concepts so they will understand and begin to embrace them in their own lives and families.

WHAT'S MISSING?

In Session One, we established the key idea that a cultural shift has occurred. The very rapid movement after World War II from an agricultural to an industrial society caught unsuspecting families in its wake. John-Boy, we're not on Walton's Mountain anymore! In fact, I believe that the Waltons' lifestyle, and that of the families in many of the cultures I encounter as I travel the globe, was much closer to the ancient paths that God designed than the way most of us live today.

Am I telling you to pull the plug on your television and computer, or move to a grass hut? Of course not! Instead, I'm referring to what I call the essential experiences—four keys for living that God designed. Although He intended these experiences to point people to a relationship with Him, they are not Jewish or Christian or Muslim in themselves. They're

ROPP: Watching kids from other cultures, in fact, was one of the main ways I learned about the dramatic shifts that affect families today. I would look at kids from other countries, and then at the kids in my youth group—the MTV-watching teens who seemed to spend half their lives in the drive-through lane at McDonald's—even at my own boys—and wonder which were more normal. I think you already know the answer. *(Rite of Passage Parenting)*

not American or Asian or African, either, although I've seen them repeated all over the world. These four essential experiences are embedded deep in the hearts and lives of the world's people because . . . God placed them there. They're an integral part of His perfect design, His ancient paths.

Read through this key Scripture once again: "Thus says the Lord, 'Stand by the ways and see and ask for the ancient paths, Where the good way is, and walk in it; And you will find rest for your souls'" (Jeremiah 6:16 NASB). Remember your English grammar? A verb is an action word! God's prescription for His people, given above, gives us four verbs that tell us the action we can take to help us follow the ancient paths. Find and list them here (group members, feel free to work together).

When our culture shifted, we left the ancient paths and moved away from providing the essential experiences that belong there. That's why our families are hurting. We've lost the skills to help our children become capable, responsible, self-reliant adults.

Let's examine the first essential experience. I discovered its importance when I noticed that young people in other cultures assumed *adult responsibilities*— including marriage, parenting, and professional jobs— and *adult consequences* at much younger ages than the young people with whom I worked in my youth ministry. I saw teenagers in Israel who carried loaded machine guns as part of their mandatory military service. I witnessed thirteen-year-olds in the jungles of Panama who already had the skills they needed for adult living. They could gather wood, prepare food, care for children, even build their own homes—and they did. They lived capable, responsible, self-reliant lives.

Our culture, however, does not typically trust its young people with responsibilities much greater than remembering to bring a bag of chips for the class party. Parents moan and sigh about the behavior of their offspring, wondering when, if ever, they will finally grow up. What happened to cause this dramatic difference between our culture and the non-westernized world? You guessed it. I traced the problem back to the cultural shift, which has pulled an ancient path right out from under our families: the path known as *rite of passage* that provides young people with a definite step between childhood and adulthood. The following diagrams help illustrate this concept.

 ROPP TERMS:

ADULT CONSEQUENCES: Predictable outcomes determined by one's own choices.

ADULT RESPONSIBILITIES: An individual's obligations to himself and to others under his authority.

RITE OF PASSAGE: A clearly defined line that distinguishes childhood from adulthood.

RITE OF PASSAGE

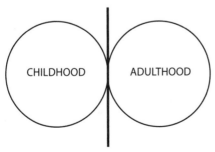

FACILITATORS: Continue affirming your group members as the good parents you know they are. Rite of passage may be a new concept for them, but because we all long to grow up, they should readily understand and identify it. Be sure to express gratitude or other positive affirmation for every individual who shares a response. Exercise discernment as you decide which of the next few questions to discuss as a group.

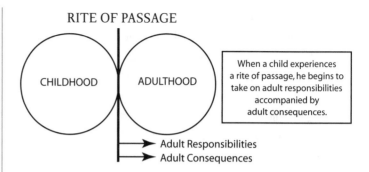

RITE OF PASSAGE

CHILDHOOD   ADULTHOOD

Adult Responsibilities
Adult Consequences

When a child experiences a rite of passage, he begins to take on adult responsibilities accompanied by adult consequences.

Today's kids do not understand when or how they grow up because our culture fails to provide them with the essential experience of rite of passage. We fail to tell them how to grow up—so, quite often, they don't.

The summer that I graduated from high school, I also joined the U.S. Army. Both events served as important rites of passage in my life, helping me to cross the line from childhood to adulthood. List below any activities or events that marked your own coming of age or into maturity, along with the age at which you experienced this event. For example: "Took a full-time job, age seventeen." "Accepted to nursing school, age twenty."

The other cultures I visited, and our culture prior to the agricultural-industrial cultural shift, either provided a formal ceremony like the Jewish *bar/bat mitzvah* to provide clear definition between childhood and adulthood, or an *informal rite of passage* like house-building embedded within the culture. Rites of passage provided young people with the means and desire to handle adult responsibilities and adult consequences, moving them quickly and definitely from childhood to adulthood. It also helped them do what many young people in our culture fail to do: grow up.

As I began learning to "fix it" by studying youth culture in the United States and elsewhere, I realized that the word *teenager* itself is a relatively new term, dating back only to the previous century. About the time that our culture shifted from agricultural to an industrial model, we also began to develop the idea of the spoiled and self-indulgent teenager, someone who was not yet ready for life as an adult.[1]

List the first three words that come to your mind when you hear the word "teenager."

Can you see it yet? Our culture has, for the most part, stopped providing rites of passage for our young people. Today's kids are missing a clearly defined way to move from childhood into adulthood.

 ROPP TERMS:

INFORMAL RITE OF PASSAGE: A distinction between childhood and adulthood marked by adult responsibilities and adult consequences rather than formal recognition through an event and/or celebration.

FACILITATORS: If possible, present the following section as a guessing game. Ask participants to close their books or lay them face-down. Read aloud one of the descriptions of the adult responsibilities taken on by the young people in "Do the Math." Have members guess the age of the one who accomplished it. To ensure that the game remains challenging, mix up the order shown here.

 FACILITATORS: Play the Bible teaching segment of the Session Two ROPPcast at this time. Whether or not you use this option, please go over the Bible teaching in the next few paragraphs and prepare to explain or read alongside your group and/or partner.

They don't know when to grow up—and, even more importantly, they don't know *how*.

 HOW IT SHOWS

✓ **ROPP BY THE NUMBERS:**

22 . . . age at which Thomas Alva Edison received his first patent for an invention, an electric vote recorder.[2]

16 . . . age at which George Washington took his first paid position as a surveyor.[3]

15 . . . age at which Walker Moore became co-owner of a photography business.

14 . . . age at which John Quincy Adams became the secretary to the U.S. Minister to Russia.[4]

12 . . . age at which Pocahontas helped the Jamestown colonists, including Captain John Smith.[5]

9 . . . age at which Wolfgang Amadeus Mozart composed his first symphony.[6]

Maybe you know the story—Luke 2:41-52. It describes every parent's worst nightmare: a missing child. Mary and Joseph were on their way home from the annual gathering in Jerusalem. Most likely, they traveled as part of a caravan, men and women walking separately. Amid the crowd of people—the dust, the confusion, and fatigue—it's no wonder it happened. Still, Mary's response was no different from the response of a mother today whose child goes missing: deep concern and mounting fear.

Jesus had disappeared! He was right there beside them—wasn't He? Suddenly, three days out of the city, His parents came to the awful realization that their son was gone. After a long night and longer trip to retrace their steps, the weary couple found Him. Scripture says that He was in the temple, "sitting in the midst of the teachers, both listening to them and asking them questions" (Luke 2:46b).

As I studied this story, I had what I always seem to have: questions. How could Jesus, the Savior of the world, ditch His parents? I know how I would have responded if one of our boys had treated Cathy and me this way. Not only that, but when Joseph and Mary found their son, He answered them almost rudely: "Did you not know that I must be about My Father's business?" (Luke 2:49b). How could these actions and answers come from Jesus, the sinless Savior of the World?

You guessed it. Essential experience #1, rite of passage, provides the answer. Jesus was not acting as a child when He stayed behind in the temple. Instead, He was responding as an adult who had gone through His *bar mitzvah*, the Jewish rite of passage, at twelve years of age. He had taken on adult responsibilities (dialoguing with the teachers and fulfilling the prophecies of Scripture) and adult consequences (making arrangements such as where He would stay and what He would eat while He was there). Jesus was acting as an adult because in His day and in His culture, He *was* an adult. When He told His parents that He must be about His Father's business, He was simply reminding them of His status and obligations. Jesus had gone through a rite of passage. Jesus had become . . . a man.

ROPP TERMS:

ADOLESCENCE: A culturally-defined term describing the period between childhood and adulthood when an individual is neither a child nor an adult.

PENDULUM OF ADULT RESPONSIBILITY: The point at which an individual assumes adult responsibilities (the obligations of an individual for his own life and for others over whom he has authority).

PENDULUM OF PHYSICAL MATURITY: The point at which an individual becomes capable of biological reproduction.

When our children begin growing up, it's easy to respond like Mary—with reluctance, fear, and even anger. Think about a time in your life when you showed evidence of growing up (example: leaving home to attend college). Write three words that describe your parents' response to that time (you may need a separate set of words for each of your parents).

As our culture began to delay the time when our children took on adult responsibilities, we invented a new term for the newly created period between childhood and adulthood: *adolescence.* I use the following diagram to explain the problem:

THE INVENTION OF ADOLESCENCE [7]

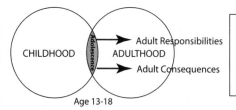

CHILDHOOD   Adolescence   ADULTHOOD   → Adult Responsibilities   → Adult Consequences

Age 13-18

Adolescence: the period between childhood and adulthood where an individual is neither a child nor an adult (a culturally-defined term that Rite of Passage Parenting believes is a false concept).

Rather than allowing our young people to follow the ancient path of moving quickly from childhood to adulthood in a clear rite of passage, the cultural creation of adolescence yields . . . confusion. Our culture heightens that confusion by sending mixed messages about how and when a child becomes an adult. Does it happen when he can drive (sixteen), or when he can vote (eighteen), or maybe when he can drink alcohol legally (twenty-one)? Today's young people don't know—and we're not doing a very good job of telling them.

I like to say that our culture's invention of adolescence set a pendulum into motion. Prior to the cultural shift, even very young teens could live as mature, responsible adults. Today, the point where young people have the skills and abilities for true maturity has caused this *pendulum of adult responsibility* to swing farther and farther away from birth. While this is happening, another pendulum has begun a gradual swing in the opposite direction. This *pendulum of physical maturity* reflects the fact that kids are experiencing puberty at a much younger age than they did a century or two ago.[8]

Is the age at which young people take on adult responsibilities and consequences really moving farther and farther away from birth? Use this space to identify a responsibility you were entrusted with as a teen or young adult that most young people would not be given today. For example, at age twelve, I ran a smelting pot that melted pig iron for a linotype machine. I also poured the hot lead into forms so they could be inserted into the machine. Yes, I still have the scars—but that man-sized responsibility prepared me to become part owner of the business just a few years later.

FACILITATORS: The questions are becoming slightly more personal now. Be careful to continue casting into your group members the idea, regardless of the comments they share, that each one is a *good parent* who is interested in learning more.

By the way—if you can't name any adult responsibilities you took on at an age others would consider young, remember: it's not your fault. You got caught in the cultural shift.

Today's young people are confused about when and how adulthood begins because our society does not provide them with a rite of passage. As a result, many of them create their own marks of maturity, trying desperately to reach adulthood through a *false rite of passage* such as smoking, drinking alcohol, body piercings, and more. These activities fail to move young people into capable, responsible, self-reliant adulthood—and so, in many cases, parents think they need to follow their kids wherever they go.

Remember our "black box dad" from the previous session? Our culture is filled with parents exactly like him. Our culture has begun to use a special term for these caring, concerned, but often too-close-for-comfort moms and dads: *helicopter parents.*

Our society's failure to provide genuine rites of passage has led many parents to hover over their kids, but it has also led to a cultural trend that continues to increase. Many of us have heard of the *boomerang generation,* young people who, seemingly unable to cope with life on their own, keep returning to the family home. Futurist Faith Popcorn has coined an additional term for these young adults who live in their childhood bedrooms: *B2Bs* or *back-to-bedroom kids.*[9] Let's examine some statistics that reveal just how quickly this trend is advancing within our culture.

CULTURE SHOCK: Since the 1970s, there has been a 50% increase in the number of young adults in their twenties living at home, which alone has led to a 19% increase in shared housing costs incurred by parents.

Although slightly more than half of men and nearly two-thirds of women had left their parents' home by age twenty-two, 16% of both returned home at some point before age thirty-five.[10]

Once a parent, always a parent. You won't suddenly stop being a mom or dad when your kids reach a certain age or milestone. The dramatic increase of the B2B trend is one more indicator of the cultural shift. But should young adults continue living at home? Circle the letter that best explains your thoughts about how long they should stay with their parents:

 ROPP TERMS:

BOOMERANG GENERATION (ALSO "BOOMERANGS"): Young adults who refuse to be self-reliant and keep returning to their authority (a designated person or persons to whom an individual voluntarily submits his will) for the basic needs of life.

B2BS OR BACK-TO-BEDROOM KIDS: Jobless or underemployed Boomerangs who have returned to their parents' homes to live.

FALSE RITE OF PASSAGE: An artificial means of marking the line between childhood and adulthood.

HELICOPTER PARENTS: Moms and dads who hover above their children because they don't think the kids are capable of handling things on their own.

a. Until they can support themselves.

b. Until they get married.

c. Until they're twenty-one.

d. Until they graduate from college and/or have a full-time job.

e. Until they have their first child—and maybe not even then.

MOMSPEAK: *I know many moms who are like me. We enjoy our children and sometimes have a hard time seeing them grow up. After all, God has built deep within us the desire to love and nurture them. He designed us this way, and His ancient path doesn't change just because our kids have gotten a little taller or their voices have changed.*

Once again, in order to embrace rite of passage for my own kids, I had to look at parenting in a fresh way. I needed to look beyond the moment to the big picture. That can be hard to see through the haze of midnight feedings, scattered Legos, birthday parties, endless chauffeuring, or whatever duties you face in your season of motherhood.

To find that big picture, I didn't have to look far—just down the street where we lived for seven years. In three different homes lived four young men, all in their late twenties or early thirties, who (as I realize now) were B2Bs. Only one of them had a regular job. The others all had plenty of extra time to talk on their cell phones, play with their big-boy toys, argue with one another and with their parents, and generally set a very bad example even in a pleasant middle-class neighborhood.

The lives of those young men contrast sharply with the hopes and prayers I have for my children's future. Moms like me may have a tough time letting go, but if it will help my kids become capable, responsible, self-reliant adults who live their lives as God intends, I'll gladly become Mama Bird.

Remember her? She prepares her children to fly . . . then pushes them out of the nest. Rite of passage? Bring it on!

ESSENTIAL EXPERIENCE #1: MARK THEIR MATURITY THROUGH A RITE OF PASSAGE

No doubt, you can repeat the familiar line from the toy store commercial: "I don't wanna grow up." Across cultures and continents, I have found just the opposite to be true: one aspect of the ancient path that God has implanted within us is the deep desire to . . . grow up. Little girls love to dress up in Mommy's clothes and high heels. Little boys valiantly push toy lawnmowers across the lawn. Kids *do* want to grow up—but, as we've seen, sometimes our culture doesn't let them.

Scripture teaches, "When I became a man, I put away childish things" (1 Corinthians 13:11). As we have seen, adults carry adult responsibilities. What responsibilities have you assumed as an adult that you did not carry as a child? Write at least three in this spot.

 ROPP: What can you do to provide closure for your kids' childhood, equipping them for life by helping them move into responsible adulthood? You already know the answer: you provide a rite of passage, a definite step between the two realms. However, you don't just wake up your child one day with the words, "The time is here. Today . . . you are an adult!" *(Rite of Passage Parenting)*

ROPP TERMS:

BREAKING POINT: The point at which scientists use the combined acceleration and new gravitational pull of a spacecraft to reset its course.

LUNAR SLINGSHOT: A scientific phenomenon that uses the gravitational pull of the moon to accelerate a spacecraft's momentum and recast its trajectory in a new direction; also known as *gravity assist.*

PRINCIPLE OF EXPECTATION: Thoughts and ideas planted in an individual's mind that help guide his future development.

RITE OF PASSAGE CELEBRATION: A formal recognition by family and friends that acknowledges the crossing over of the line between childhood and adulthood.

As a concerned and frustrated youth minister who had begun to study the ancient paths set forth in Scripture, I realized that a time would come in every child's life when it would need to be recast. I would need to work with parents to help them push their child toward a definite break with childhood, accelerating into a more adult orientation. As I developed these ideas, I learned about an amazing phenomenon that scientists call the *lunar slingshot,* pictured here:

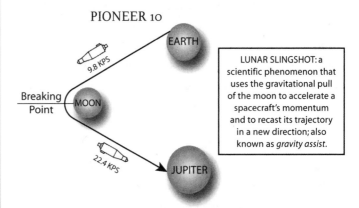

PIONEER 10

LUNAR SLINGSHOT: a scientific phenomenon that uses the gravitational pull of the moon to accelerate a spacecraft's momentum and to recast its trajectory in a new direction; also known as *gravity assist.*

Scientists use this phenomenon, in which the gravity-drawn spacecraft accelerates until it reaches a *breaking point,* to "slingshot" the craft away from the surface of the moon or other heavenly body, increasing its speed and changing its direction all at once. Once I understood this, I began to use the model of the lunar slingshot to explain the definite, dramatic, life-changing effect that a rite of passage has on an individual's life.

Ideally, this process begins as soon as you know your child has been conceived. Even then, you can begin taking specific steps—*rite of passage preparation*—that will help prepare him to grow toward capable, responsible, self-reliant adulthood.

We'll talk more about those steps as we continue working through the ROPP material.

Let's begin with what ROPP calls the *principle of expectation*, which states that the thoughts and ideas planted in an individual's mind help guide his future development. As a Rite of Passage Parent, you will use this concept from your child's earliest days to cast the expectation into him that one day, he will grow up— and that later, you will call forth his rite of passage. He will want to grow up because you will have spent time throughout his life speaking to him about this ancient path and telling him again and again about the capable, responsible, self-reliant adult he will become. He will want to leave his toys behind because you have repeatedly spoken with him about the exciting adult responsibilities he will take on when he becomes . . . a man.

Whether or not you realized it, you have been preparing your children to become adults since the moment they were conceived. That's because you're a good parent! List two things in this space that you have taught your child/children that will serve them the rest of their lives.

RITE OF PASSAGE EVENT: A step that moves an individual quickly and definitely from childhood to adulthood.

RITE OF PASSAGE PROCESS: A series of incremental tasks designed to build adult responsibilities into an individual's life, preparing him for the transition from childhood to responsible adulthood.

There comes a time, as we said when I was growing up in rural Missouri, when it's time to stop petting the mule and hitch up the wagon. Like the spacecraft in the lunar slingshot, your child will one day reach a breaking point that shoots him off in a new direction. Now, he is ready to cross the line, turning away from childhood and accelerating into adulthood with its adult consequences and responsibilities. For your children, this breaking point is the life-changing experience that ROPP calls a *rite of passage event.* Here's the ROPP Diagram I used to illustrate this.

RITE OF PASSAGE PARENTING

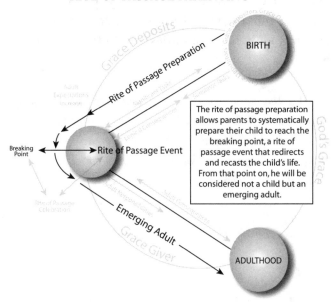

Without a clear rite of passage event at the time of their breaking point, kids experience confusion and the rebellion that often accompanies it. That's a vulnerable time because so many of them begin to seek out false rites of passage—inappropriate and often dangerous attempts to grow up. A genuine rite of passage frees them to move into adulthood in healthier ways. At this point, we don't consider them adults, but *emerging adults* whose lives have moved away from childhood and are making definite progress toward adulthood. They have crossed the line into adulthood by experiencing a meaningful rite of passage event.

I suggest that each family decide on an appropriate rite of passage event for a particular child (see the list of ideas in Fix-It #2-1 on page 59). Parents can best determine an event that will call forth each child's adulthood, making sure it includes adult activities and responsibilities. No matter how worthwhile the event may be, a child who merely follows instructions without completing adult activities such as initiating, organizing, and carrying it out will not experience a genuine rite of passage.

When I realized that a rite of passage was missing from the lives of so many teenagers, I began incorporating international mission trips into my work with students. Eventually, I left my position as a youth minister to found Awe Star Ministries, www.awestar.org. I designed this organization specifically to provide rites of passage by giving young people the opportunity to take on adult tasks and responsibilities through short-term international ministry (see the additional information about Awe Star in Fix It #2-2).

Once our student missionaries surrender to laying down their adolescence, Awe Star begins treating them as adults by building adult tasks and responsibilities into their lives. On the field, the students take charge of transporting our sound system, first-aid kit, and properties box to every drama site—with no reminders from leadership. Each one manages his own money and schedule, again without reminders and urgings from leadership. We have seen radical, even immediate, transformations in students' lives by holding them to adult expectations. Here's how that looks in our ROPP Diagram:

RITE OF PASSAGE PARENTING

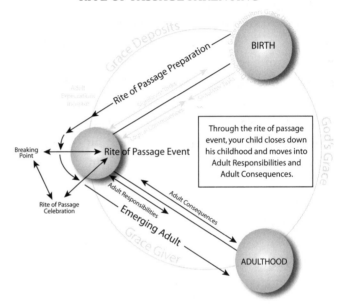

Through the rite of passage event, your child closes down his childhood and moves into Adult Responsibilities and Adult Consequences.

Use the following space to list some of the adult responsibilities for which you want to prepare your children. For example: paying bills, driving and maintaining a car, planning and cooking a family meal.

I make no apologies for the fact that I believe in Awe Star Ministries. However, ours is not the only avenue by which you can provide your children with a rite of passage event. As a Rite of Passage Parent, your commitment is not to Awe Star, but to God and to your family. Continue to seek Him as you look at returning this important experience—an integral part of the ancient path—to your family. Mom and dad, your kids *do* "wanna grow up" because He has instilled that desire deep within them. How they get there is largely up to . . . you.

After a young person completes a rite of passage event, I suggest that families affirm God's work through a *rite of passage celebration.* This observance tells the world that the emerging adult has accomplished certain significant steps, displaying the evidence of her adulthood for the emerging adult, her family, and everyone else who witnesses it. See the suggestions for a rite of passage celebration in Fix-It #2-3 on page 60 (Rite of Passage Celebration Planning Form) and #2-4 on page 62 (Rite of Passage Celebration Template).

DADSPEAK: *When I was a child, I lived outside of the small, rural community of Buckner, Missouri. I attended a tiny country church there called Six Mile Baptist. You have seen churches just like it—little, white, framed buildings, a tiny cemetery in the back. The church was named "Six Mile" because it was located six miles outside of Fort Osage. Some of my fondest childhood memories trace straight to that humble country church.*

As I reminisce, I have tried to understand why those days hold such powerful, pleasant memories. Part of my personal delight stems from the way the men of the church let us young boys work alongside them. I remember when we needed to build an educational building. I was just ten—maybe twelve—years old, but when the "men" gathered to raise this building, Dad took me along. I helped pull the electrical wires, swept the floors, and pushed wheelbarrow-loads of cement.

A boy gains a certain satisfaction when he does a man's job, especially when he is referred to as one of the "men." I remember dragging my little body home, thinking I couldn't move another step. Of course, this exhaustion only lasted until my brother asked if I wanted to play baseball.

A few years later, that same educational building burned down due to electrical problems. I have always wondered if my wiring had anything to do with it! Nonetheless, the men of Six Mile Baptist helped me move toward capable, responsible, self-reliant adulthood by, even at that early age, calling me . . . a man.

Do you remember a time in your life when, at a young age, someone referred to you as a man or woman? If so, you understand in part how affirming a rite of passage celebration can be. Write a few words here that remind you of one of the first times someone acknowledged your adult behavior.

As I travel the country teaching these principles, parents often ask me questions like this: how do we really know that emerging adults *are* adults—and how do we help them reach that point? You could write an entire book about that, and I have: *Rite of Passage Parenting! ROPP* teaches five marks of maturity taken from Scripture that will help you move your child through his rite of passage: "Do not let anyone treat you as if you are unimportant because you are young. Instead, be an example to the believers with your words, your actions, your love, your faith, and your pure life" (1 Timothy 4:12 NCV). Check Fix-It Form #2-5 on page 63 for specific ideas about the five key areas that can help you and your child navigate a rite of passage successfully.

One young man who exemplified these qualities was BJ Higgins. I tell part of his story in *ROPP*. Be sure to read his dad's words here. They explain a little more about what a rite of passage event looks like in the real life of a real young man.

WHAT ARE THE ODDS? One thing I especially remember is speaking to BJ on the phone. He said to us, "Mom, Dad, I know when you dropped me off for this trip [a five-week missionary journey to Peru], you dropped off a boy. I just want you to understand that a change has taken place. When I come home, I'm coming home a man."

When we got off the phone, Deanna and I laughed and joked together, "Yeah, BJ's going to come home a man. He can't remember to feed the dog or empty the trash, he can't remember to start his homework before he plays video games, but he's coming home a man . . ."

We traveled to St. Louis to pick him up. We walked into the hotel lobby where his team was assembled.

They were giggling, but we didn't initially think too much about that: We were very anxious to see our BJ. We looked back over the crowd, and the snickering grew to outright laughter. I remember looking at Deanna and saying, "Why are they laughing at us, and where is BJ?"

About that time, my eyes fell on him, standing in the center of the group. We did not recognize him because his physical appearance had changed completely! His hair had grown long, and, at the age of fourteen, he had grown a full beard.

The Lord [used] the physical changes in his body to reflect the real change in his spiritual, mental, and emotional nature. While he had been away, he really *had* become a man. Certainly, there were times where he had lapses and failures, but we did see a marked change in how he approached things. His attitude toward his mother was now very helpful, and he also became very focused spiritually. It was definitely a turning point.—Brent Higgins, Sr.[11]

I know you remember that you're a *good* parent! I'm proud of you because you have already processed so much of this material and dealt with such life-changing concepts. Before we go on to the devotions for this week, I want to have you consider one more question that will serve to remind you that not only are you a good parent—you have some great kids too!

Pretend that your oldest child is standing in front of you—whether that oldest child is five months old, five years old, or thirty-five years old. Now, imagine yourself standing in front of him or her and saying, "I'm so proud of you! You're growing up! I know this because I see

_____ *in your life." Fill in the blank by*

writing down two different areas in which you see evidence of maturity there. If you need a quick review, look over the Marks of Maturity in Fix-It #2-5 on page 63.

 51 PERCENT: This week, concentrate on the following ROPP handles:

1. Deep within our hearts, God has imbedded the desire to grow up. Many children's favorite toys or games center around this longing. This week, look at your own children. Use this space to list some of the toys they play with or the games they play that tell you . . . they want to grow up! (Parents of older children or adults can answer for their own children at younger ages, and those who are childless or the parents of infants can answer for children they know well.)

2. If you had to decide today on a rite of passage event to slingshot your oldest child into adulthood when he reaches an appropriate age, use this space to list or describe two possibilities that you would consider. (If you have an older child who has already experienced a rite of passage event, make sure to write it here as well.)

DO NOT TRY THIS AT HOME . . . YET. I ask that no good parents begin casting the vision for a rite of passage into his or her children before completing Session

SPECIAL NOTE: some of you may have realized by now that your own life has been caught in the shift. Maybe, even though you've reached physical maturity, you can't really be considered a capable, responsible, self-reliant adult. Or maybe, even though you're grown with a family of your own, your parents still treat you like an irresponsible child.

If you find yourself trapped in one of these ways, please begin to pray about your own rite of passage. Ask God to give you an opening into a conversation with your parents or other adults who have taken on a parental role in your life. He can make a way for them to help you mark your maturity. If you know Him as your Father, He can pronounce your adulthood when He sees that you are ready. He is waiting. Just ask!

Five of this book and/or reading Section Four, "Grace Deposits," of *ROPP*. Just . . . keep reading!

3. If you have the opportunity, read and/or review Essential Experience #2: Significant Tasks, chapter 4–6 in *Rite of Passage Parenting.*

4. Over a five-day period before beginning the next lesson, read and study the five-day ROPP Devotion Guide that follows the Fix-Its for this session. Next, complete the following: *Each of the ROPP devotions for this week addressed the concept of rite of passage from a slightly different angle. Which one meant the most to you, and why? Write its title here along with a few words that remind you what God said and how you responded.*

FIX-IT #2-1
SUGGESTED IDEAS FOR A RITE OF PASSAGE EVENT

CAMPING TRIP: A weeklong, away-from-home camping adventure for parent and child. The child should plan the date, arrange the place, gather all supplies, and organize the activities. If possible, he or she should also earn money to pay for at least a portion of the trip.

COMMUNITY SERVICE: An extended period of time in which the child sacrifices his or her time in order to help others such as the homeless, children with long-term illnesses, etc. In order to serve as a rite of passage event, this activity must be one that the child plans, initiates, organizes, and carries out—not simply one where he or she participates in a previously organized program.

SENIOR ADULT ADOPTION: A relationship that the child initiates with a senior adult. The child will plan activities for the two to do together, assume adult tasks with which the senior adult needs help, and make him- or herself available for extra responsibilities as they arise.

WORSHIP SERVICE: An event that the child plans, organizes (including music, Scripture, message, and prayers) and executes, taking personal leadership in as many areas as possible.

INTERNATIONAL MISSION TRIP: An extended time in which the child leaves his or her culture and travels overseas to minister to others. In order to serve as a rite of passage event, the trip must be designed in such a way that the child has the opportunity to take on adult tasks and adult responsibilities. In the lives of thousands of students, this has been proven more effective than any other rite of passage event. See Fix-It #2-2, Awe Star Ministries.

FIX-IT #2-2:
AWE STAR MINISTRIES, GENERAL INFORMATION

Why send your child on an Awe Star Global Passage? We are one of many sending organizations who are passionate about reaching the lost for Christ. In many ways, we are all the same. We all target certain people groups. We all have connections with local missionaries. What is the Awe Star difference?

The answer is very simple: Awe Star is just as interested in equipping young people for life as we are in bringing new life to a lost world. In short, the difference lies in the teaching we pour into our missionaries. We are passionate about raising a generation that can stand on its own two feet—one that will go against the flow of a culture that says the Christian life is all about convenience. Awe Star wants to equip young people with the tools to surrender their desires and futures to Christ.

Repeatedly, Awe Star has been recognized as the source of the most advanced discipleship training that students ever receive. As we prepare our missionaries for the field, we also equip them for life by teaching them to understand the Word and will of God. Our discipleship covers everything from spiritual warfare to identity in Christ. Our missionary service includes opportunities for students to take on adult activities and responsibilities including managing their own time, money, and witnessing opportunities.

Everyone returns from the mission field with great stories. When students complete an Awe Star Global Passage, they return with much more. An Awe Star Global Passage is a rite of passage event. This means the Awe Star difference lasts . . . for life.

www.awestar.org

1-800-awe-star

FIX-IT #2-3:
RITE OF PASSAGE CELEBRATION, PLANNING FORM

The emerging adult should be involved in the planning of this celebration as much as possible. Unless the service itself will serve as his rite of passage event, he does not have to take complete charge of planning it. However, an essential component is his rite of passage testimony, in which he speaks as an adult to share about his rite of passage event. If father, mother, or both are unavailable to serve as designated here, the EA will need to choose other significant figures to carry out their roles in the celebration.

OPENING PRAYER: Given by a person who has had a meaningful relationship with the Emerging Adult (hereafter abbreviated EA) and chosen specifically by the EA for this role in the ceremony.

RITE OF PASSAGE OVERVIEW: Brief explanation of the concept of a rite of passage by the EA's pastor, parent, or other participant.

MUSIC: Hymns or other spiritual songs. Flexible; may add more music elsewhere in the service if music is important in the EA's life. The EA should choose the music and participate in a significant way by leading a song, sharing why it has particular meaning, etc.

RITE OF PASSAGE TESTIMONY: A critical element consisting of words prepared by and delivered from the EA about the rite of passage event, spoken as an adult using appropriate attire and communication skills.

RITE OF PASSAGE CHARGE: Time in which those in attendance at the celebration will have the opportunity to affirm the EA using words such as: "I know you're ready to accept your adult responsibilities and consequences because . . . " This allows the EA to hear from others that he is ready for a rite of passage, reinforcing the ancient path that is being called forth and holding him accountable for the future through the principle of expectation. The charge concludes with an affirmation and charge from the mother and then the father, who leads in bestowing a special gift such as a sword bracelet, ring, or other outward symbol of emerging adulthood to mark the EA's rite of passage.

RITE OF PASSAGE SURRENDER: Symbolic representation in which the EA moves from one side of the room to the other, joining the same-sex parent and other men or women as he or she crosses the line from childhood to adulthood. This may be followed, if desired, by the celebration of communion by the EA and the group of men or women.

RITE OF PASSAGE BLESSING: Time in which the father lays hands on his EA and prays. This prayer of blessing releases the EA into adulthood, confirms him or her as a man or woman, and calls forth positive character qualities in the EA through the principle of expectation.

CLOSING PRAYER: Given by an adult who has a meaningful relationship with the EA, chosen by the EA to perform this role.

FIX-IT #2-4:
RITE OF PASSAGE CELEBRATION, TEMPLATE

Rite of Passage Celebration, Emerging Adult (EA)

Day, Date, Year

Opening Prayer	Significant adult chosen by the EA
Rite of Passage Overview	Pastor, Parent, or other significant adult
Music	
Favorite Praise Chorus	Brother, Sister, or other relative
Favorite Hymn	All
Rite of Passage Testimony	EA
Rite of Passage Charge	Mother
	Father
Rite of Passage Surrender	EA and Father and other men (for a young man) or EA and Mother and other women (for a young woman)
Rite Of Passage Blessing	Father
Closing Prayer	Significant adult chosen by the EA

FIX-IT #2-5:
Marks of Maturity: Moving Toward Adulthood

Speech:
- Do I communicate with people of all ages clearly and respectfully?
- Does my speech reflect others' interests, desires, and needs rather than only my own?
- Do I use my words to build others up?
- Do I use my words to confess sin and seek forgiveness when appropriate?
- Do my words reflect what is true, right, pure, and holy?

Actions:
- Do I act in a way that points to Christ's authority in my life?
- Am I striving to seek God's glory in everything I do?
- Do my actions reflect eternal rather than temporary values?
- Do I seek to "die daily," surrendering myself and my desires to Him?

Love:
- Do I seek to serve others, putting their needs ahead of my own desires?
- Do I give and serve without thought of return?
- Do I seek the good of others rather than myself?

Faithfulness:
- Have I surrendered my time and desires to Christ?
- Do I keep my promises?
- Can others count on me to willingly, carefully fulfill my obligations?

Pure Life:
- Have I sought to remove all bitterness (which can lead to corruption) from my life?
- Do my words and actions reflect that my body is a temple of the Holy Spirit?
- Do I seek to take every thought captive to the obedience of Christ?
- Do I renew my mind with the Word of God?
- Have I surrendered my sexual purity to God's standards?
- Do I have others who hold me accountable for purity in thought, word, and deed?

RITE OF PASSAGE PARENTING
DEVOTION GUIDE

DAY 1: PREPARED TO BE RESPONSIBLE

READING: *The prison warden chose Joseph to take care of all the prisoners, and he was responsible for whatever was done in the prison. The warden paid no attention to anything that was in Joseph's care because the Lord was with Joseph and made him successful in everything he did* (Genesis 39:22–23 NCV).

OBSERVATION: When both of our boys were in college and living on their own, they thought they were self-reliant. Now, you have to realize that my definition and my sons' definition of "living on your own" and "self-reliant" are worlds apart. I must have an older dictionary.

Yes, they were living away from our house, but *not* on their own, and yes, they knew how to find food. Instead of going to the grocery store like every other self-reliant human being, they somehow believed that if they came over, looking sad and hungry, Cathy and I would feel sorry for them . . . and they were right.

Because we were good (and hopefully godly) parents, we always fixed them care packages, and the boys loaded up their cars, driving away with smiles of delight. I had mixed feelings. I liked the fact that they still needed us, but deep down inside, I wanted them to become self-reliant.

As your children prepare to live "on their own," be prepared to answer these questions:

"How can you tell when an egg goes bad?"

Suggested response: "When something starts pecking its way out of the shell, the egg is probably past its prime."

"How can I tell when the yogurt is bad?" At this point, go ahead and answer about three more questions just to save on your phone bill.

"Milk is spoiled when it starts to look like yogurt. Yogurt is spoiled when it starts to look like cottage cheese. Cottage cheese is spoiled when it starts to look like regular cheese. Okay?"

"Okay."

"Remember these rules: Any canned item that has become the size or shape of a softball should be disposed of . . . carefully. Fresh potatoes do not have roots;

branches; or dense, leafy undergrowth. Flour is spoiled when it wiggles. Now you know everything I know about food. Good night, son!" Click.

All humor aside, too many of our children will not become self-reliant and must move back home. A recent study showed that 61 percent of all college graduates have plans to become Back-to-Bedroom Kids, moving back home under their parents' support.[12]

Many of today's young adults have lost the skills of independence and self-reliance. They even expect their parents to take care of *their* children and help pay *their* bills.

When I finished high school, I knew my days of dependence were numbered. The problem is that no one has cast this same expectation into this generation.

What did I like best about my sons coming home from college for the summer? I got to see my food again!

PRINCIPLE: Begin to prepare your children now to become capable, responsible, and self-reliant adults.

PRAYER: *Lord, I love my children—but I want them to grow up. Help me begin now to give them skills for living. Help me to raise not children, but . . . adults. Amen.*

DAY 2: HANKIES AND KLEENEXES

READING: *So he walked in all the ways that his father had walked; and he served the idols that his father had served, and worshiped them. He forsook the LORD God of his fathers, and did not walk in the way of the LORD* (2 Kings 21:21–22).

OBSERVATION: Were you like me? Did you hate it when your momma wiped your nose? If your mother was anything like mine, she thought words like "soft" and "gentle" were reserved for commercials.

In fact, I believe Rudolph became "The Red-Nosed Reindeer" only after his mother repeatedly wiped his nose. If you had given my mother a Kleenex and put her in the ring with a snot-nosed professional wrestler, she would have had him pinned before he knew what had hit him.

Looking back, I realize that there were several things that I considered rites of passage. One of these was getting my first wallet. Something about having a wallet makes a young boy feel grown up. Even with a cowboy's picture stamped on the outside and a zipper to seal it shut, it was still a man's wallet and held a dollar bill.

Carrying a hanky also made me feel grown up. In those days, every capable, responsible, self-reliant adult had a hanky. Grandma's and Mom's were white and lacey. Grandpa's and Dad's were checkered red and white. One Christmas, I got a package of three child-sized, white hankies. No longer did my momma need to wipe my nose—I was now taking responsibility for anything it produced. I stood with a sense of emerging adulthood—wallet in one hip pocket, white hanky in the other.

I tried to continue these traditions with my sons. They took the wallets and the dollar bills, but to this day, they absolutely *hate* hankies. They can't imagine why anyone would blow mucus into a square piece of cotton, fold it, and carry it around in a back pocket or purse for a day. I, on the other hand, don't leave home without my hanky. The generation gap still exists. Today, I am on the other side of it.

As parents, we need to realize that things change. Using a Kleenex instead of a hanky is neither right nor wrong. Remember not to make an issue out of something just because it is . . . different. Ask God to show you the things that are essential, and set an example your children can follow in those areas.

I used to say I wanted to be buried with my hanky in my back pocket, but I've changed my mind. Instead, I am going to leave my hanky collection to my sons. After all, my estate is . . . nothing to sneeze at.

PRINCIPLE: Sometimes, the choices our kids make are not wrong, just . . . different. Ask God to help you pass the essentials on to your children so they can follow . . . Him.

PRAYER: *Father God, please lay on my heart the truths that need to be passed from generation to generation. Help me pass on the ancient paths rather than the cultural trends—and give me the wisdom to know the difference. Amen.*

DAY 3: I NEED AN ORGANIZER

READING: *Therefore, I urge you, brethren, by the mercies of God, to present your bodies a living and holy sacrifice, acceptable to God, which is your spiritual service of worship* (Romans 12:1 NASB).

OBSERVATION: I read recently that three out of four business travelers carry a Palm Pilot. You have probably seen someone using one of these tiny, hand-held computers. People like this have their entire life stored within its depths . . . in alphabetical order, cross-referenced by zip code. Just ask them a question. They whip out their personal wizard from a hidden pocket and start punching away.

Ultra-organized individuals like this derive great satisfaction from seeing their entire life catalogued on a miniature screen. Then there are people like . . . me. God has given me wonderful skills, talents and gifts, but organization is not among them. I have a desk that has not seen daylight since man walked on the moon.

I married one of those organized people. I fall to my knees every day, thanking the Lord for a wife who helps me keep my stuff together. She has a Palm Pilot. I do not. Although I own more personal organizers than the average human being will use in three lifetimes, I can never seem to find them. So I began to consider investing in a Palm Pilot.

A recent Sunday sales flyer listed all the marvelous things that Palm Pilots can do. It boldly claimed capacity for 12,000 addresses, four hundred e-mail addresses and . . . wait a minute! Who has 12,000 addresses? More appropriately, who *needs* 12,000 addresses? I added up the entries in my address book. Grand total, one hundred eighty-one—and I don't even know who some of them are. Adding my doctors' addresses will bring me to one hundred eighty-three. If I add the plumber, the mechanic, and the pizza delivery number, I can move up to one hundred eighty-six. I only need 11,814 more. My hometown does not have that many names in the entire telephone book!

I have to ask myself a very hard question. Is an organizer something I *need* . . . or just something I *want*?

The Lord reminded me that most of the world's people do not have their needs met, let alone their wants. The ways in which God has met our needs should make our wants seem insignificant every time.

Besides that, if I ever did get one of those electronic organizers, it would quickly be lost somewhere in the bottom of a drawer . . . just like the old-fashioned kind.

Principle: Teach your children to know the difference between *wants* and *needs*.

Prayer: *Father, I know that my children will learn by looking at my life even more than by listening to what I say. Help me to live in such a way that when they examine what I do, they will see that I know the difference between wants and needs. Amen.*

Day 4: Steak and Shake

Reading: *For He has strengthened the bars of your gates; He has blessed your children within you* (Psalm 147:13).

OBSERVATION: I can remember the day, but not the year. Somehow, the older I get, the more those years get confused.

I'm sure I remember the exact day . . . because it was Jeremiah's birthday. I felt sorry for him. We were driving the eight hours from Grandma's house in Hannibal, Missouri, all the way home to Tulsa. No child should spend his birthday in the back seat of a car. How could I make this day special?

As we approached Springfield, I remembered a "Steak 'n Shake" restaurant there. Now, Jeremiah loves few things more than meat. As a boy, I saw an episode of *Mutual of Omaha's Wild Kingdom* that showed a cow wading into a river. Within ten seconds, a school of piranhas ate the poor animal clear to the bone. Watching Jeremiah eat meat brings back that episode—in living color.

I asked him, "Do you know what a man should have on his birthday?"

He stared back at me, wondering. "No, Daddy, what?"

"A steak. A big, juicy steak . . . that is what a man should have on his birthday."

I could sense the wheels spinning inside his small head. "It's my birthday. I am a man. That means I should have steak today."

My next words made the wheels move even faster. "That's not all, Jeremiah. Do you know what else a man should have?"

"What's that, Daddy?"

"A shake. A thick chocolate shake to wash down that steak. That is what a man needs on his birthday: a steak and a shake."

By now, his little wheels were turning double-time. The only thing that Jeremiah consumes faster than meat is chocolate. I could see his thoughts: "Today is my birthday. I am a man. I should celebrate with a steak and a shake."

I spoke once more. "Jeremiah, would you do me a favor? I need to keep my eyes on the road. Could you please watch for a place that serves steaks and shakes?"

At this point, Jeremiah was leaning over the back seat, straining to find that special place. I knew that in a mile or so, we would reach a sign with directions to the restaurant. Every fifteen seconds I would ask, "Have you found anything yet?"

It's a good thing I anticipated the sign. When Jeremiah caught sight of it, he screamed at the top of his lungs, "Look, Dad—a place that sells STEAKS AND SHAKES!" "Good! Let's go there and celebrate your birthday!"

Jeremiah is now thirty years old. Recently, he asked me, "Dad, you remember when we ate at "Steak 'n Shake" for my birthday?"

Of course, I did—although I'm glad he didn't press me about the year.

"Dad, what you did . . . that was pretty cool."

I just smiled.

PRINCIPLE: Put blessings into your child's life by creating memories that will return to you as a blessing in the future.

PRAYER: *God, help me today to see opportunities to put blessings into my child's life. Allow those blessings to grow and multiply so that they return to those who bless them, even . . . me. Amen.*

DAY 5: NOW, WE RUN

READING: *For the LORD your God is bringing you into a good land, a land of brooks of water, of fountains and springs, that flow out of valleys and hills* (Deuteronomy 8:7).

REFLECTION: A grandfather, out for his daily walk, noticed a small boy trying valiantly to reach the doorbell on a house down the block. After watching his effort for some time, the grandfather stepped smartly across the street, walked up behind the little fellow and, placing his hand kindly on the child's shoulder, leaned over to give the doorbell a solid ring. Crouching down, the old man smiled benevolently and asked, "And now what, little man?"

The boy replied, "Now, we run!"

Oh, the dilemmas of parenting! It was not too long after our second son was born that I began to pray seriously for Christ's return. Some days, I wanted to resign from fatherhood altogether. I felt like saying to my wife, "Now, we run!" The only thing that saved our children from becoming orphans was that, fortunately, my wife and I never had this thought on the same day.

Every parent wants to raise a capable, responsible, self-reliant child. Still, something within us makes us feel good when he or she turns to us for help. We never want to feel that our child can live without us. One of the most difficult choices of parenting occurs at the intersection of "help" and "do not help."

I believe there are two parenting extremes: "Butterfly" parents and "sea turtle" parents. At the very first sign that their child is struggling, "butterfly parents" run to help, trying to remove the problem. In nature, if a fully-developed butterfly is removed from its cocoon prematurely, it will never fly. It gains its strength by fighting its way on its own. In the same way, children who are not ever allowed to make mistakes or struggle grow up unprepared to handle the difficulties they will face in life.

The "sea turtle" parent presents just the opposite pattern. The sea turtle, after laying its eggs on the beach, leaves them to hatch on their own. Some parents leave their children to raise themselves without any assistance, nurturing, direction, or love. These children, treated with indifference, usually become "sea turtle" parents themselves.

God has placed the ancient paths within us so that we would continue seeking His wisdom and direction. When we find these truths, we can adopt them, look at one another, and say, "Now we run" . . . in God's direction.

PRINCIPLE: Confidence in parenting comes from the Word of God—the perfect portrayal of God's ancient paths.

PRAYER: *Dear Father, teach me how to be a parent. Help me to seek Your Word so that it will become a light and lamp to guide me in raising my children. Amen.*

SESSION THREE

∽

SIGNIFICANT TASKS

GOALS, SESSION THREE:

1. Learners will understand and identify the need to provide children with *significant tasks* (activities that demonstrate your value and worth to the people you consider important).
2. Learners will begin to embrace the idea that, as good parents who seek the "ancient paths," they will want to provide age-appropriate simulator and significant tasks for their children.
3. Learners will begin to develop practical ways to provide their children with both simulator and significant tasks in their own homes and families.

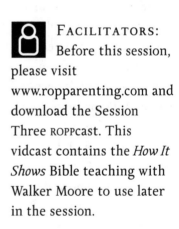

MAKE YOURSELF AT HOME

By now, I'm sure you remember my son, Caleb. In *ROPP*, I tell the story of the day that I was working (or at least attempting to work) on our car—the one given to our family by one of the deacons in our church—the one that was always breaking down. As I banged away on the old

FACILITATORS: Before this session, please visit www.ropparenting.com and download the Session Three ROPPcast. This vidcast contains the *How It Shows* Bible teaching with Walker Moore to use later in the session.

FACILITATORS: As the group gathers, ask God to make you sensitive to the needs of each member. Encourage them to begin sharing their responses to question #1 in the 51 Percent homework from Session Two (page 57), dealing with toys or games that demonstrate "I wanna grow up!" Remind them that since God has implanted this ancient path deep within our children, even the way they play demonstrates this innate longing.

As members begin to share responses, stop and pray—or have a group member pray—for your time together. Supplement the discussion as needed with suggestions from your own list of "grown-up" games, toys, or suggested rite of passage events. Continue through the remaining 51 Percent questions as time and group dynamics allow. Group Facilitators may choose to review the ROPP Contract (Fix-it #1-1, page 25) with the group as well.

rattletrap one Saturday morning, four-year-old Caleb stopped by our garage. He peered down at me, his mouth forming those three little words that dads (sometimes) love to hear: "Can I help?"

Could Caleb help? Well, not much. Not at four years old, anyway. However, even I, the guy who doesn't always get it right, knew better than to throw away this opportunity. Caleb, like each one of us, had a need to know that he mattered, that the things he did had real value—especially to his mother and me, the most important people in his small world. I handed him a screwdriver and asked if he could keep it from rolling away while I worked. Caleb could . . . and he did. Not long afterwards, a proud young man stood in our kitchen, puffing out his little chest and happily telling Cathy, "I helped Dad fix the car!"

Did you grow up like Caleb, "helping" your dad fix the car? Maybe you liked to "help" Mommy feed your baby brother or shop for groceries. Use the space below to record two childhood memories in which you "helped" an adult perform an important function. For example, my grandfather and namesake, Walker Winfield Scott, loved to attend auctions. Grandpa allowed me to "help" him bid by holding up his special auction cane—the same one that stands proudly beside my front door today.

WHAT'S MISSING?

I bet you've already figured it out. Caleb's "helping" me fix the car, my "helping" Grandpa place a bid at the auction, and whatever "helping" you accomplished as a child all fulfilled a part of the ancient path that God has placed within us. His distinctive design makes this "helping" especially important in our lives. In fact, His ancient path is the reason that people from generation to generation and culture to culture seek assignments that they deem meaningful. We all yearn for something special to do that demonstrates our worth and adds value to our family or others we consider important. Each one of us naturally seeks Essential Experience #2, what ROPP calls a *significant task.*

My conversations with thousands of students through the years have verified this deep desire for significant tasks. Today's young people not only long to grow up, they long to make a difference—to do things that truly matter.

Perhaps that explains why, when I asked a large group of former students what part of my teaching had the most impact on their lives, they couldn't give me an answer—at least, not the kind I wanted. I wanted what any youth minister longs to hear: my expounding and expanding on the truths of God, my direct and personal teaching, had changed their lives forever. Instead, they told me something that continues to shape my ministry today: the Bible studies had helped prepare them, but what had changed their lives forever were the experiences and opportunities they had gained in serving overseas.

These students had, for short periods of time, left their culture behind and taken on new responsibilities—responsibilities for managing their own health and

 ROPP TERMS:

SIGNIFICANT TASK: A special assignment that demonstrates an individual's worth to the people he considers important.

 ROPP: By its nature, an agricultural society gives every child significant tasks that make him feel important and valued. . . . Prior to the agricultural-industrial cultural shift, however, the average child brought his family the equivalent of five thousand dollars in annual income. Back then, children were a necessity, not a luxury, because they quickly learned practical skills and took on important responsibilities. *(Rite of Passage Parenting)*

belongings, but, even more importantly, for touching and changing the lives around the world. What counted, as far as these students were concerned, were . . . significant tasks.

*Significant tasks matter to people of all ages because they are a part of the ancient path that God has instilled within us. In the past, we chose our heroes based on their significant tasks: Roy Rogers fought the cattle thieves. Superman saved the city from destruction. Today, we tend to have **idols** rather than heroes. We grant god-like status to rock stars and athletic champions regardless of their character and lifestyle.*

Have you ever had a true hero? If so, list the name of at least one of them and his or her significant task below.

FACILITATORS: Sharing the answers to the next question should generate some lively discussion! Plan to use a whiteboard or posterboard on which to list heroes and their accompanying significant tasks. Affirm group members for their growing understanding of this concept as you continue through the session.

I believe that today's young people find tasks like these especially meaningful because, in their everyday lives, most of them feel useless. What they do just doesn't count—and they know it. Over and over, when I ask students what they do that gives them worth or adds value to their family, I hear the same answers: "I make my bed." "I take out the trash." Typically, even if they are involved in a youth ministry program at church, their tasks are no more significant than bringing the Cokes or passing out the pencils for the weekly fellowship time. This devalues them as individuals and teaches them to accept—and expect—a low level of responsibility.

One of the reasons so many young people today end up hopeless, helpless, and useless is that no one has allowed them to perform tasks that count beyond the moment. Instead of depending on little Johnny to chop the wood so we can heat our home, or little Susie to churn the butter or bake the bread so we can have food for the table, we stick them both in bedrooms equipped with the latest CDs, DVDs, MP3s, and TVs. Later on, we wonder why—even in their twenties or thirties—they never want to leave. They have not become capable, responsible, self-reliant adults because no one has equipped them by giving them significant tasks.

The need for this essential experience is so great, in fact, that an individual who has no significant tasks typically takes on what ROPP calls *pseudo-significant tasks*. These tasks remind me of the false fronts on the Hollywood movie sets. Although they outwardly appear to have meaning, when you pull aside the façade and look behind them, you find no real house, no real store, no real . . . significant task.

An everyday example of a pseudosignificant task is our country's current fascination with kiddy sports. Please don't misunderstand me: these sports can certainly serve a good purpose. The problem comes through too many parents spending too much time shuttling their children from one practice to another game to another lesson to another practice, all in the futile search for significant tasks. In our post-cultural shift world, we don't know how to provide our kids with the significant tasks they seek, so we outsource

 ROPP TERMS:

PSEUDOSIGNIFICANT TASKS: Activities that outwardly appear meaningful but have no intrinsic value.

that responsibility to the peewee football team, the soccer coach, or the cheerleading instructor.

This sports problem extends past our kids and their overloaded schedules, though. You've read the stories: Dad goes berserk at son's football game. Mom comes unglued when the soccer referee makes a bad call. Why this obsession? Since the cultural shift, kids' sports activities often become pseudosignificant tasks for parents who lack significant tasks of their own.

Nearly all of us have take on pseudosignificant tasks at one time or another. As reflectors of culture, the characters in television shows and movies mirror this truth. For example, much of the humor in the old "I Love Lucy" series centered around Lucy's search for significant tasks. She ran around selling Vitameatavegamin, stomping grapes, or trying to convince Ricky to let her perform at his club *just once* because, deep down inside, she longed for (you guessed it) significant tasks.

Think about the characters in your favorite movies or television shows, present or past. Do any of them perform pseudosignificant tasks the way Lucy did? Take a few moments to list one character and his or her pseudo-significant tasks below.

FACILITATORS: You may want to answer the following question as a group. Continue affirming members as good parents regardless of their answers. Praise them for learning to recognize rite of passage and significant tasks, as well as the counterfeit pseudosignificant tasks. They have already absorbed a lot of new material just in getting to this point, so make sure to tell them you appreciate them because they are good parents who are willing to work hard to become better ones.

How It Shows

ROPP BY THE NUMBERS:

190,528 . . . average number of dollars U.S. parents spend to raise a child from birth to age 18 (2004 figures).

136,800 . . . average number of dollars U.S. parents spend to raise a child from birth to age 18 (1960 figures).[1]

527 . . . average number of hours a year that U.S. parents spend helping their 18-to-20-year-old offspring with chores (2006).[2]

25 . . . percent of all young adults 18–34 who are not a part of the labor force (2006).[3]

If you haven't understood anything else about ROPP up to this point, I hope you see that times really have changed. Statistics like the ones you just examined bear this out. Today, we're raising a generation of young people who are *more* dependent and *less* responsible than at any time in the past. That means they are moving farther and farther away from the ancient paths God has placed within them—the paths that give each one of them an innate desire to grow up, to do something that matters.

Jesus Himself exemplified these ancient paths. Although He was fully God, He came to earth as a tiny, helpless baby. He moved forward into capable, responsible, self-reliant adulthood through a rite of passage—the one the Jewish people call *bar mitzvah*.

FACILITATORS: Facilitators who downloaded it will want to play the Bible teaching segment of the Session Three ROPPcast at this point in the study. Whether or not you use this option, please go over the Bible teaching in the next few paragraphs and prepare to explain or read alongside your group and/or partner. As time allows, plan to play another high-low game with the statistics given here. Have your group members close their books, then divide into two teams. Turn each statistic (use rounded numbers if you prefer) into a question, for example, "According to 2006 figures, how much money did U.S. parents spend to raise a child from birth to age 18?" Ask Team 1 the first question. Members will discuss it among themselves before giving an answer. Now, take this answer to Team 2 and ask if they believe the correct response is "higher" or "lower" than what their counterparts said. After giving the right answer (and allowing more discussion time if needed), present the second question to Team 2 and allow Team 1 to vote "higher" or "lower" for the answer they give. Continue through all four statistics if time allows.

He showed His adult status during His time at the temple in Jerusalem, where He remained behind to take on adult responsibilities and adult consequences when His parents began traveling back home. But Jesus did something more during that sojourn in Jerusalem. The passage in Luke 2 also describes the very first time that Jesus, during His time on earth as a man, took on . . . significant tasks.

At just twelve years old (still a lowly "preteen" by today's standards), Scripture says that Jesus "amazed" the temple teachers with His understanding and His answers (Luke 2:47). But what made His task significant was the fact that had He not been there, He would have sinned.

Jesus—sin? If Jesus had sinned, He could not have been the spotless sacrifice that God required. If Jesus had sinned, He could not have been the Savior. And if Jesus had not been the Savior, everyone from Adam and Eve to the last person on earth, would have died and gone to hell—with no hope of redemption. That makes twelve-year-old Jesus' time in the temple a *very* significant task.

But Walker, I can hear some of you saying. *How do you know that if He had not been there, He would have sinned? How could that one little episode in the temple have mattered so much?*

I know it mattered so much because Scripture clearly says that it did. Look with me again at Jesus' answer to His parents. He tells them that He was carrying out His heavenly Father's business—the very first recording of what He later described as His pattern of doing "exactly what the Father told me to do" (Luke 2:49 NCV). Had Jesus not stayed behind in Jerusalem to learn, listen, and eventually speak in the temple, He would have failed to carry out His Father's will. The Bible has just one word for that: sin. Had Jesus sinned, we would have lost our sinless Savior— and we would have been lost for eternity. That's why I can say with confidence that Jesus' time in the temple that day was nothing less than a *very* significant task!

Everyone needs to be needed! If you listen to a group of senior adults talk for more than a minute or two, you'll realize that they love to talk about the good old days. Often, the good old days were the days when they all had (you guessed it) significant tasks. Think of the senior adults you know and the topics they enjoy discussing. List three or four of them here, marking an S beside each one that involves a Significant Task.

 ROPP: Educator Stephen Glenn reminds us that all people have a well-defined "need to be needed" that is often stronger than the need to survive. When Caleb asked to help fix the car . . . he was showing his need to be needed. He wanted to have a place of value and worth in his family. When we fail to give our children Significant Tasks, this need goes unmet.

However, as Glenn notes, children are not the only ones who need to be needed. As he points out, research shows that adults who view themselves as fulfilling an important role in society produce more, experience better health, and recover from illness more quickly than those who believe their work is insignificant or unimportant. *(Rite of Passage Parenting)*

CULTURE SHOCK: Finally researchers have come up with a reason other than pure laziness for why teenagers can't shower and brush their teeth or unload the dishwasher and wipe down the counter.

Blame it on "cognitive limitations." Their brains can't multitask as well as those of the taskmasters. . . . The part of the brain responsible for multitasking continues to develop until late adolescence, with cells making connections even after some children are old enough to drive, according to a new study in an issue of the journal *Child Development*. . . . Unfortunately the study did not reveal any solution to parents at their wits' end over the problem. But [the researcher] did offer this advice: "We need to keep their cognitive limitations in mind, especially when adolescents are confronted with demanding situations in the classroom, at home, or in social gatherings."[4]

In agricultural societies, children begin moving toward adult responsibilities from the moment they are born. I've watched this in culture after culture. The Embera Puru begin preparing for their rite of passage event, house building, from the time they can pick up sticks or carry grass. The Karamajong of Uganda leave their eight-year-old sons in charge of their family wealth—the cattle—when the fathers go off to hunt. The Choco, deep in the jungles of Panama, provide every one of their tribe members, regardless of age, with a significant task—from bark-stripping to leaf-chopping to fire-stirring to (as I experienced while I lived among them) alligator-hunting. In these societies, what you *do* defines who you *are*. In our culture, more and more of our young people struggle to find their identity because they have no idea what they *do*.

Today, the pseudosignificant tasks that young people take on to make up for the lack of this essential experience look different than those of the sign-waving, protest-marching students of the 1960s. Multitasking teens carry on multiple instant-messaging conversations while alternately playing a computer game and writing on their Weblog, talking on a headset, or text-messaging. These young people use technology to seek affirmation, value, and meaning for their lives. They increasingly turn to these substitutes for significance because they realize just how *in*significant their lives and their activities have become. (And apparently, no one has informed them about the "cognitive limitations" that the experts say will prevent them from multitasking!)

Even when the rare young person tries to take on adult tasks and responsibilities, culture comes alongside them to say, in effect, "You can't do that—you're just a kid!" We have added so many rules and restrictions to our children's lives that they have a harder and harder time leaving childhood behind. No longer can little Johnny "buck" (a special way of using the knee to flip an object) bales of hay onto the wagon as I did at my grandparents' farm—he might get hurt. No longer can little Susie stay home from school to help with a family crisis—she might not get into the perfect college.

I enjoyed performing the significant tasks that my grandparents assigned me. Did you have grandparents (or adults in your life other than your parents) who gave you important responsibilities even at a young age? If so, write down their names and some of the tasks they gave you.

When our culture shifted and we lost basic skills for survival, even adults began to drop responsibility for more and more of the things they had always provided for their families. Today, we outsource everything from our family's entertainment (which now belongs to Nintendo, Play Station, and Disney) to nutrition (McDonald's, Burger King, and Stouffer's take care of that) to educational and spiritual development (we expect schools and churches to cover these areas of our children's lives, often without our input).

God placed the ancient path of significant tasks within us. His purposeful design teaches us to take responsibility for our own lives. When we don't provide significant tasks for ourselves or our children . . . it shows. ROPP wants to help you take a step backwards and examine your own responsibilities for the areas that our culture has taught you to outsource. I consider that a significant task.

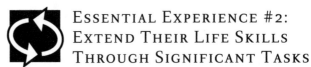 ESSENTIAL EXPERIENCE #2:
EXTEND THEIR LIFE SKILLS
THROUGH SIGNIFICANT TASKS

God has specifically designed His ancient paths to help parents guide a child from helpless infancy into capable, responsible, self-reliant adulthood. This represents a path toward . . . freedom. Following the ROPP principles will help you return to the ancient paths and build that same freedom into your family's life. Gradually, as kids take on first one significant task, then another, then another; parents will find release from responsibility for their care. That's freedom!

But how do we reach that point? We no longer live in an agricultural society. Most of us have no reason to teach little Johnny to haul and stack the wood so that one day, a bigger Johnny can chop the logs, split them, and build the fire himself. How, then, can post-cultural-shift moms and dads build skills for living into our kids' lives?

The answer comes through a process that involves gradual, step-by-step preparation for responsibility. God uses this same incremental process. When we demonstrate that we can be faithful with "a few things," He is willing to trust us with "many things" (Matthew 25:21, 23).

As a kid back home on the family farm in Missouri, my parents and grandparents gave me chores. These were smaller, significant tasks that prepared me for bigger ones. They added worth and value to my life because I knew that my efforts helped my family. They also helped prepare me to perform larger tasks and take on greater responsibilities as I grew older.

I have coined a term to describe this crucial and gradual preparation: *simulator tasks*. A friend of mine who trains commercial pilots tells me that they all begin their training in a flight simulator, gradually building the abilities they will ultimately use in the real aircraft. Even the most experienced pilots periodically return to the simulator to sharpen their skills. Here's what simulator and significant tasks look like as part of the ROPP diagram we've been building (next page).

Simulator tasks are important. In fact, during our childhood, simulator tasks are ... significant. Like Caleb holding the screwdriver while I worked on the car, simulator tasks prepare us to take on greater responsibilities as we mature. Can you name a simulator task you've given one or more of your children, preparing him or her to take on greater responsibilities? Name at least one of these simulator tasks in the space on the following page.

 ROPP TERMS:

SIMULATOR TASKS:
Sequential, developmental activities that build skills for living and prepare the one who performs them to undertake significant tasks.

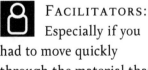 FACILITATORS:
Especially if you had to move quickly through the material that led up to this point, make sure group members understand the basic definitions of simulator and significant tasks before attempting the following question.

RITE OF PASSAGE
SIMULATOR AND SIGNIFICANT TASKS

BIRTH

Rite of Passage Preparation

Significant Tasks

Adult
Expectations
Increase

Simulator Tasks

Breaking
Point

Rite of Passage Event

Through simulator and significant tasks, a child learns the skills to become a capable and self-reliant adult.

Rite of Passage
Celebration

Emerging Adult

ADULTHOOD

DADSPEAK: *Some of my best memories from my childhood come from times spent with my grandfather and namesake, Walker Winfield Scott, my first hero.*

Being a boy, I loved things that were sharp and dangerous. Grandpa always used an old-fashioned, long-handled sickle to cut the grass next to his long driveway. He walked up and down, back and forth, swinging his shining sickle in a seemingly effortless rhythm.

In a matter of moments, he would have a quarter-mile of tall grass smoothly sheared. Swinging a sharp blade and instantly seeing the grass go flying? How cool was that? My fingers itched to try my hand at his method of mowing.

For a long time, Grandpa refused to teach me to use the sickle. I'd take it and whack away at that grass, trying to emulate his actions, but I only succeeded in bending the grass as I swung the sickle awkwardly across it.

While I whacked, Grandpa worked. He sat there for what seemed like hours, sharpening the blade of another sickle with a metal file. I couldn't understand what he was doing, or how sharpening just one blade could possibly take him so long.

Finally, one day, he brought me over and sat me down beside him on an old tin bucket. My lesson began with his words: "Walker, the secret in mowing is not in the way you swing the sickle. The secret lies in the preparation."

Grandpa taught me everything he knew about filing those blades—and that was a lot. I can't count the number of times I watched him patiently working away on the rough edge of a hoe or shovel, honing and rehoning the edge until he got it exactly right. If you entered his workshop, you noticed immediately that every tool hung sharp, shiny, and ready to assist him.

Grandpa taught me much more than the basics of tool-sharpening, though. He taught me that, in order to succeed in my work, I needed to maintain my equipment. More importantly than that, he taught me the lifelong lesson that the success of a job is only equal to the preparation behind it. I learned never to skip that important step—a principle that has served me throughout my life.

When you give your kids simulator tasks, remember that you're teaching far beyond the moment. The skills are important—but the principles endure . . . forever.

MomSpeak: *There's no doubt about it. Walker and I bring different perspectives to ROPP. He's a dad. I'm a mom. He and Cathy have two grown sons. Tom and I have, as he likes to say, "all boys . . . except for four girls."*

Another area where Walker and I differ is that his sons attended public school, but our family homeschools. What could that possibly have to do with significant tasks?

I have always included "life skills" in my homeschool lesson plans. The change of seasons and clothing always prompts a life skills session. Each child has learned to sort, fold, and organize clothing in closets, dressers, and storage areas. In addition, every few months, we cook and freeze between forty and fifty main dishes. At these times, we use school time to work together in planning, shopping, and meal preparation. My son has learned to build a fence, change the oil in the car, and accomplish other household tasks as part of his studies. Yes, my children have daily jobs that aren't a part of formal school, but homeschooling provides flexibility to teach important life skills when appropriate.

You may have guessed it by now. "Life skills" are simulator tasks that prepare the Pieper children for significant tasks. In fact, their growth toward capable, responsible adulthood is one of the reasons I can take time to work on writing projects like this one!

Of course, you don't have to be a homeschooler to give your kids simulator tasks. Keep reading and applying the ROPP essential experiences in your own family life. Watch the smiles on your kids' faces when they succeed at a task because you've taken time to train them well. Before long, you'll experience the even greater miracle of watching their lives transformed as they travel overseas (or wherever God leads them) and take on tasks that are truly . . . significant.

When we give our kids simulator tasks that build toward significant tasks, we are building on a very important foundation—not of skill or knowledge, but *desire.* We need to capitalize on the "Can I help?" attitude kids tend to exhibit in their early years before it becomes the "Do I *have* to?" of a rebellious or indifferent teenager. The rite of passage preparation process, as shown in the previous diagram, includes this gradual, step-by-step preparation through the use of simulator tasks. This adds skills and abilities to the foundation of desire, ultimately preparing the child to take on significant tasks.

Factors like birth order, affluence, level of education, and family size affect the way parents assign simulator and significant tasks to their kids. *Mark this statement True or False and be ready to explain your answer.*

Jesus provided the perfect example of this method of instruction when His disciples asked Him to teach them to pray (Luke 11:1). First, Jesus *modeled* prayer, doing exactly as the Father had taught Him, and the disciples eagerly watched. Next, He began to *instruct* them with the knowledge and skills they needed. After that, He prayed right *alongside* them so they could watch and understand His teaching. Finally, He encouraged them to pray *on their own* as He watched.

As Cathy and I began to build skills for living into our sons' lives through simulator tasks, we followed this same method. Of course, it's the one I encourage you to apply as you begin equipping your kids for life. In Fix-It #3-1 (page 92), you'll find an example that shows how to walk out this method as you teach a child to perform a simulator task. Fix-It #3-2 (page

ROPP: We've all seen mother birds patiently teaching their babies to fly. In our day, we follow the opposite pattern. At a certain point, we kick our children out of the nest and expect them to fly—without any simulator training. We haven't taken the time to build significant tasks into their lives. Since our overgrown baby birds have spent no time on simulator tasks, they have no skills for living. Small wonder that many end up as boomerang or B2B kids. (*Rite of Passage Parenting*)

96), contains lists of age-appropriate simulator tasks that can gradually build into significant tasks. Stop and take a quick look at these examples now before answering the following question(s).

Parents sometimes fail to assign significant tasks because they fear the mistakes their children will make. However, God can use our mistakes and failures to teach great lessons. Use this space to tell about a mistake you made when performing a simulator or early significant task. For example, maybe you overfilled the washer and caused a laundry room flood—or burned one of the first dinners you tried to cook. Share a mistake here along with a short summary of the lessons you learned through it.

♥ WHAT ARE THE ODDS? The spring that my daughter, Jami, was fifteen, she came home from a conference where she had heard about Awe Star Ministries. She and I had been on a church mission trip the summer before. Now, she had such a great desire to go on an international mission trip with this organization that she could not keep quiet!

I'm a homemaker, and my husband had recently begun a commission-based job. She needed between four and five thousand dollars for the trip. Not only that, but she had heard about the trip so late that she had only two weeks to raise the money. We were tempted to make her wait for another year, but we agreed as a family that God could be the fall guy this time.

Jami spoke to our church, and within forty-eight hours, God had provided the entire amount she needed. Everyone was shocked! We never imagined that our church would be willing to give so much.

When she got back from her thirty-day trip, we were amazed at what God had done. Awe Star had given each team intensive training before leaving the country. During this time, our daughter laid down her adolescence. She was told, "From here on, you need to realize that everything you do affects others—not just yourself."

Jami saw God work in deep ways. She learned to depend on him for great and small things. She came back so much more confident in God and in herself. He showed her how significant her task really was: if she didn't go, who would? She began recruiting her friends to serve as Awe Star missionaries, too. Jami has since followed him to serve with Awe Star in several other countries.

Awe Star does missions right. They will work you until you think you can give no more—and then you do. It's like the show "Survivor," but with a purpose that's so much more meaningful.

Jami's mission trips with Awe Star have changed not only her life, but our family, our church, and our friends. We have all seen God do amazing things through her signifcant tasks. —Tammy Layman[5]

We all know that parenting has moments of frustration. List one or more conflicts that occur in your home because your child/children do not behave as capably or responsibly as you would like. (Example: I argue with my daughter because she leaves the bathroom a mess after she takes a shower).

 51 PERCENT: This week, concentrate on the following ROPP handles:

1. When we taught our boys to take on simulator tasks, we first had to break the process down into incremental components (see Fix-It #3-1 and #3-2 on pages 92 and 96). This week, take one of the simulator tasks that you hope to teach your child and break it down this same way. Write the name of the task and a step-by-step description of how to do it here. DO NOT TRY THIS AT HOME . . . YET. I ask that no good parents begin teaching simulator tasks to their children before completing Session Five of this book and/or reading Section Four, "Grace Deposits," of *ROPP*. Just . . . keep reading!

2. If you have the opportunity, read and/or review "Essential Experience #3: Logical Consequences," chapters 7–9 in *Rite of Passage Parenting*.

3. Over a five-day period before beginning the next session, read and study the five-day ROPP Devotion Guide that follows the FIX-ITs for this session. Next, complete the following: *I began the book by telling you about how I intended to "make myself at home." I bet you've noticed some remodeling or redecorating already! Which devotion did the most "rearranging" in your heart this week? Write its title below, along with a few words about why you found it especially meaningful.*

FIX-IT #3-1:
SIMULATOR TASK TRAINING: PAYING A BILL

ROPP: We can apply the same steps Jesus used, with minor adaptations, to almost any simulator task we need to teach our kids. In fact, I recommend applying those same steps to significant tasks. (*Rite of Passage Parenting*)

When our son, Jeremiah, was about nine years of age, Cathy and I decided to use the process of bill-paying as a way to begin building adult skills and responsibilities into his life through a simulator task. Although we taught him to pay our electric bill using a checkbook, the same method is adaptable to paying other bills and even to online payment; substituting the computer, mouse, and Web site for the checkbook, pen, and stamped envelope. I recommend following a process like the one described below.

DO NOT TRY THIS AT HOME . . . YET: Before you take your child through this process, and before you teach her to perform any simulator or significant tasks, you will need to study and understand Section Four, "Grace Deposits" in *Rite of Passage Parenting*, or Session Five of this workbook.

STEP 1: MODELING—PARENTS PERFORM TASK WHILE CHILD WATCHES

Before modeling payment, help your child understand the basic concept of a *bill.* Explain that when we use something, we must pay for it. When we go to the grocery store, we pay for the food we bring home. At the discount store, we pay for the shampoo, toys, or other items we purchase. The more these items cost, the more money we have to pay.

With commodities that we use every day like water, gas, and electricity, we pay for what we use too. The same rule applies: the more we use, the more we pay. Each company has a special way to measure the amount used, and they send us a statement every month called a *bill.*

At this point, let your child examine your electric or gas meter. You might even watch for the meter reader and let the child observe him moving from house to house.

You may also have to explain the concept of a *check* to your child. Perhaps you have had the experience (as almost every parent has) of explaining that you couldn't afford something, only to hear his words: "Then just write a check (or use the ATM)." This attitude needs correction before she becomes an adult. In fact, before she is ready to pay a bill, a child must understand the concept of a checking account, including that funny little rule they have down at the bank: you must deposit more money than you withdraw. Unless the account contains the money to cover it, a check has no real value. Show the child your checkbook and register to help her make the connection between deposits and checks written. If you wish, you can also show her examples of checks written to pay other household bills.

Next, you need to build into your child the *desire* to pay the bill. You do this by communicating the importance and value of this significant task. Emphasize that bill paying is an activity that every adult must learn, and that you are trusting her with a very important part of your household finances. Discuss what could happen if she failed to pay the bill (for an electric bill, this would mean no lights, no television, no computer use, etc.). You might even schedule an "electricity free day" where the family experiences a sample of life without electricity (or other commodity, depending on the bill) in the house as a whole, in the children's bedrooms, or elsewhere. Also, make sure your child understands that if she fails to pay the bill and the electricity gets cut off, she will have to use her own funds to pay the reconnect fees.

STEP 2: INSTRUCTION: PARENTS EXPLAIN EXACTLY HOW TO PERFORM TASK

Show your child the actual bill. You will probably want to designate a special box or basket to place it in for her to retrieve after it arrives in the mail. Point out the different parts of the bill: company name, family name and address, account number (an abbreviated way to show exactly which house the bill belongs to), date and amount used, cost, last year's usage, and the perforated section that allows you to send in a stub and keep a receipt.

Next, carefully demonstrate the entire process of paying the bill: examining it to determine the amount owed, filling out the check except for the signature, recording the amount in the check register and subtracting it from the balance indicated, getting the signature from a parent, placing the check and payment stub in the envelope, stamping and mailing it, and filing the bill appropriately. Another aspect of bill paying—scheduling the payment—should also be covered in your instruction time. Help your child make a calendar note or other reminder of when the bill needs to be paid.

At this point, you may want to make a "practice" check and bill so your child can experience a trial run. This exercise will help her gain confidence as she prepares.

Step 3: Child Performs with Parent Alongside

Now that you have modeled and instructed your child, she is ready to try bill paying with you close at hand. Sit beside her and allow her to go through the entire process explained above, being careful to make it a time of affirmation rather than rebuke. If she does make a mistake, affirm and then gently correct her.

When she can demonstrate that she understands the entire process and can fill in the right blanks on the check, complete the registry, perform the subtraction, and mail the bill with appropriate postage, she is ready for the next step. You may have to wait a few months before your child is ready to perform independently. However, once she has demonstrated proficiency in these skills, she is ready for you to release her to the final step.

Step 4: Child Performs Task on Her Own

You have faithfully taken your child through the steps toward paying a bill. She has completed the simulator task and is now ready to take responsibility for paying the bill on her own: a true significant task. That does *not* mean that you remind her of the assignment every day or even every week. Instead, you release her to full responsibility. On her own, she retrieves the bill from the box or basket where you place it, schedules its payment, obtains the checkbook, notes the balance to make sure the check will clear, and completes every other aspect of bill paying as explained above.

At this point, consistent and specific affirmation from mom and dad becomes the crucial component of your input. Schedule family meeting times to discuss simulator and significant tasks and other issues of family concern. Make sure these business meetings are also positive times of affirmation. Allow your bill-payer to give a report of her progress and even, if appropriate, the family's progress toward lowering expenses by turning off lights and appliances. Remember, DO NOT TRY THIS AT HOME until you have worked through the material in Session Five, "Grace Deposits," and/or read Section Four, "Essential Experience #4: Grace Deposits" in *ROPP.*

As your child grows in responsibility, she will apply the skills and principles learned from paying one bill to other areas of her life through a process called *transference of learning.* Jeremiah's life demonstrated this. He continued taking responsibility for the electric bill throughout his years at home. As he grew, we taught him other skills and principles by giving him other simulator tasks that led to significant tasks. With each one, we followed through the same process of modeling, instruction, performing alongside us, and performing on his own. When Jeremiah was just seventeen, Cathy and I lived overseas for several months. He was able to run our household entirely on his own. He attended school, kept the bills paid, and generally covered nearly every other responsibility of an adult homeowner very capably. His simulator tasks had prepared him to take on significant tasks and equipped him . . . for life.

FIX-IT #3-2:
SIMULATOR TASKS GROUPED ACCORDING TO AGE

NOTE: This list of suggestions is intended to provide general guidelines and/or suggestions only. Remember, you're a good parent who knows your child. Please apply these in an appropriate manner based on each child's individual level of development and maturity.

PRESCHOOLERS (STARTING AT ABOUT AGE THREE) CAN BEGIN TO
TAKE RESPONSIBILITY FOR:

FINANCES: Give tithes and offerings; save a portion of money received

HOUSEHOLD MAINTENANCE: pick up and organize toys or other items; straighten own bedroom; perform simple dusting; wipe appliance fronts; empty wastebaskets

LAUNDRY: sort by color; help load washer and/or dryer

MEAL PREPARATION AND CLEANUP: wash and dry fruits and vegetables; prepare simple snacks; retrieve items from pantry or refrigerator; set table; wash and dry unbreakable dishes

PET CARE: feed and brush; help exercise

VEHICLE MAINTENANCE: remove trash from interior; help wash windows and exterior

ELEMENTARY STUDENTS STARTING AT ABOUT AGE SIX CAN BEGIN TO
TAKE RESPONSIBILITY FOR ALL OF THE ABOVE PLUS:

FINANCES: pay bill(s); set up and maintain simple budget

HOUSEHOLD MAINTENANCE: maintain dresser or other drawers; more advanced dusting; vacuum; clean shower, sink, tub, and toilet; wipe kitchen counters; wash door frames, light switches, and walls; wash windows; sweep porches; clean and organize pantry; sweep and mop floors; take out trash; empty dishwasher; perform simple repairs; clean and organize basement, garage, and/or storage areas; rake and bag leaves or grass clippings

LAUNDRY: measure detergent; read clothing labels and sort laundry and dry cleaning accordingly; wash, dry, fold, and put away clothing; organize and store clothing as seasons change

MEAL PREPARATION AND CLEANUP: plan and prepare meals; take responsibility for one or more household staples (plan, purchase, maintain stock)

Pet Care: wash; groom; exercise; remove waste

Vehicle Maintenance: clean and wash (interior and exterior); wax; schedule and keep records of regular maintenance; perform simple maintenance activities such as oil changes

Emerging Adults (Starting at about Age thirteen) Can Begin to Take Responsibility for All of the above Plus the Following:

Finances: supervise household budget or a portion thereof; manage college savings

Household Maintenance: paint interior and exterior; maintain fireplaces and gutters; perform repairs (simple plumbing, carpentry, and drywall)

Laundry: iron clothing; perform laundry for other family members as needed

Meal Preparation and Cleanup: take regular responsibility for preparing family meals

Pet Care: take responsibility for health: schedule veterinary checkups and shots; administer medicine as needed

Travel: plan family or personal trips; purchase tickets; obtain travel documents; map route; obtain discounts for attractions and/or restaurants; drive for personal or family errands as well as vacations

Vehicle Maintenance: perform more extensive repair and/or maintenance activities

RITE OF PASSAGE PARENTING DEVOTION GUIDE

DAY ONE: MAKE YOUR KIDS TAKE SHOP

READING: *Go to the ant, you sluggard! Consider her ways and be wise, Which, having no captain, overseer or ruler, provides her supplies in the summer, and gathers her food in the harvest* (Proverbs 6:6–8).

OBSERVATION: I confess to you that I am a failure when it comes to my children's education. It is embarrassing to confess this to the world. I do not even understand how I got so far off track. I woke up one day and realized a horrible truth: My sons never took Shop.

When Jeremiah and Caleb were young, we enrolled them in magnet schools. Supposedly, this would give them an advantage when it came time for college. At these magnet schools, they received the most up-to-date, innovative teaching. Cathy and I thought we were being good parents, but both our boys made it through high school without taking even one Shop course. I understand most high schools still offer Shop, but I never hear about anyone actually taking it.

In my high school, every young man took either Shop or Auto Mechanics. I loved Shop! While my classmates were turning out walnut ashtrays and salad bowls, I made my parents a solid maple, seven-drawer dresser (really!).

Today's students take more unusual, intellectual classes. Jeremiah took Meteorology. He can describe a dozen different cloud formations and waxes eloquent on the subject of barometric pressure. Caleb, on the other hand, took Photography. One son can tell you when it is going to rain; the other can take pictures of the rain; but neither one can fix the roof. They do not know how to use a hammer—so what good is all that information? My boys' diplomas sit on their desks. Neither one knows how to drive in a nail to hang the thing up.

Oh, they know how to wire up a Nintendo game or splice the cable TV from one bedroom to the other. They can hook up the multiple wires on back of their computer, connect the mouse, the modem, the monitor, the scanner, the keyboard, and a host of other paraphernalia. . . but changing a burned-out light bulb extends far past their range of domestic ability.

Now that my sons are grown, all I hear from them is, "Dad, can you fix my car?" "Dad, our faucet is dripping." "Dad, the toilet is stopped up." Somewhere in all those years of education, someone should have taught them how to use a plunger.

I'm thankful both my sons earn a good salary. Someday, it will take all their money to hire someone else to do the "dad jobs" for them! Take my advice: make your kids take Shop.

PRINCIPLE: Your child becomes capable when knowledge and skill are evenly balanced.

PRAYER: *Dear Father, help me to impart to my children the tools of knowledge, then teach them how to use these tools. May the knowledge they grasp become as a scalpel in a skillful surgeon's hands. Thank You for giving me the skills I need to be an effective parent today. Amen.*

DAY TWO: LANGUAGE LESSONS

READING: *That the man of God may be complete, thoroughly equipped for every good work* (2 Timothy 3:17).

OBSERVATION: Mom and Dad, please make sure your child learns another language . . . fluently. When I was growing up, we had few chances to hear foreign languages spoken by native speakers. We may have taken four years of Spanish in high school—but we still couldn't carry on a conversation.

America is changing. God is bringing the world to our doorstep. Every day, we have opportunities to learn. I'm working to improve my Spanish. In fact, I'm convinced that the Hispanic culture must be the most advanced in the world. I run into it everywhere I turn. It seems to have penetrated nearly every area of my life.

Driving home late at night, I turn on the radio and hear, "Domingo, Domingo, el cinco de Julio!" As I flip through the channels, I hear only static and an inaudible English word or two. I hit the "search" button again to hear an accordion and a trumpet blaring "La Cucaracha." I have to come to the conclusion that either (1). My radio was made in Mexico using some secret technology that causes it to stop only on Spanish-language stations; or (2). Hispanic stations' transmitters are extremely powerful, because after nine o'clock, their signals are the only kind my car radio can receive.

Recently, while flying home from Florida, the Spanish language bombarded me once again. Wearily, I boarded the plane and reached for the ever-entertaining airline magazine—in Spanish. All I could make out was "Domingo, Domingo . . . ." Then the soundtrack for the safety movie began: "Bienvenidos a Delta." (At least it didn't say anything about "Domingo".)

As we become a global community, learning another language is more and more essential. Don't stop there: once you have learned a second language fluently, the third and fourth come much more easily.

If you want your child to get ahead, introduce another language at an early age. Visiting a Mexican restaurant is a good way to begin. Allow your child to greet the waiter in Spanish and learn the words for each item on the table. Add to his vocabulary every time you visit. Almost always, people who come from another country love helping others learn their language.

My Spanish is improving. My sons laugh at me because I sit engrossed in Hispanic TV programs. At least now I can say a few words . . . "Domingo, Domingo, el cinco de Julio; éste Domingo!" SI!

PRINCIPLE: In today's global community, becoming fluent in a second language is an important skill for living.

PRAYER: *Lord, help me equip my children to live in a changing world. Help me to teach them another language—but first, help me teach them about . . . You. Amen.*

DAY THREE: WORLD'S GREATEST PAPERBOY

READING: *And whatever you do, do it heartily, as to the Lord and not to men* (Colossians 3:23).

OBSERVATION: I grew up in a small town—the kind you have traveled through a thousand times, but can't recall. Allow me to refresh your memory.

My hometown had a main street, a bank, and a grocery store. Across the street from the grocery store was the gas station and mechanic's shop. No one visiting our town during the month of July could miss the red, white, and blue bunting draped everywhere.

Here in our town, everyone knew everyone else's name—in fact, there was at least a 50 percent chance they were related. No one ever met a stranger. Even if you were just passing through, someone would either wave or nod his head just to say, "How are you?"

One of the things that used to drive outsiders crazy was the way we all gave directions using the names of homes where people once lived. We might say, "Go down to the old Jones place and take a left." Now, no one could remember how long the Jones family had been gone, and the current owners had occupied the place for over twenty years. Still, when you asked where they lived, even the "new" residents had learned to respond, "We live in the old Jones place."

One of my first jobs was delivering newspapers. After all, if I wanted some money, I had to earn it. In the morning, I threw the Kansas City *Star*, and after school I threw the Chillicothe *Constitution-Tribune*.

Mornings began at five o'clock. When the alarm clock went off, I stumbled out of bed, threw on my clothes, slung my "paper bag" over my shoulder, and headed out to pick up my load. Some days, I walked; and at other times, I rode my bike. I cherished that rare feeling . . . moving alone through the morning silence.

My parents and grandparents raised me to believe that a job worth doing was worth doing well. I took pride in knowing that in a few more minutes, people would be getting up, putting on the coffee, opening the door to pick up the paper I had thrown, and settling down to read the news. Some would be job-hunting, and others just soaking in the headlines. Some would be scanning for a birth announcement; others, poring over the obituaries. Still others would hunt for sales or coupons to help them save money. A world of wonder, all delivered daily by . . . your local paperboy.

PRINCIPLE: Teach your children that every job is more than a job. They should approach every task as though working for . . . Jesus.

PRAYER: *Thank You, Father, for the gift of work. Help me teach my children to work hard and well, remembering that You are the One we serve. Amen.*

DAY FOUR : I HAD BAD PARENTS

READING: *"Look!" he answered, "I see four men loose, walking in the midst of the fire; and they are not hurt, and the form of the fourth is like the Son of God"* (Daniel 3:25).

OBSERVATION: I was backing out of my driveway the other day when I saw a young boy riding his bicycle. He wore more protection, head to toe, than a goalie in a hockey game: helmet, elbow guards, gloves, and more. He could not have been safer had he been sandwiched between two mattresses held together by a band of duct tape.

My parents must not have loved me nearly as much. They let me learn to ride a bicycle without any safety equipment! Yes, they would put me on a rusty secondhand bicycle, run with me for about ten feet as it gained momentum, and then let go. I would wobble along for a few feet and then crash. If I wasn't seriously hurt, we would immediately repeat the same scenario.

After many scrapes, crashes, and bruises, I finally learned to pedal in an upright position, but it took a little while (and many more crashes) before I learned to use the brakes. Good parents certainly wouldn't have allowed their child to learn via this "crash and burn" method.

But that's not all. My parents would allow the kids in our neighborhood to play that violent game, dodgeball, against our garage wall. Yes, they would allow other children to throw the ball hard, knocking us boys off our feet. When we came in crying, we got about one second of sympathy. Then we were told to get back against the wall and take our hits like . . . a man.

The horror doesn't end there. My parents drove us in cars without seat belts, airbags, or even . . . air conditioning. If we wanted to cool off, we just stuck our heads out the car window. (Until Burma Shave came along with that sign: *Don't stick your head out too far . . . it might go home in another car).* My bad parents didn't even hand out bottled water. They actually allowed the whole neighborhood to line up in our front yard and drink out of the same water hose! How unsanitary was *that*?

I'm lucky that I made it through childhood and all these dangerous activities. My parents' philosophy? If it hurt me too badly, I wouldn't do it again. They didn't make my brothers and me wear safety goggles or protective clothing. They just gave us a familiar warning: "Be careful."

Yes, according to many people, I had bad parents. If they were still alive, I should probably sue them for their lack of protection. Instead, I thank God that they allowed me to take risks. I don't believe I would be where I am today without this dangerous upbringing.

After all, where would the world be if God the Father, knowing the risks, hadn't allowed His son to come to this earth? I'm thankful . . . He did.

PRINCIPLE: As parents, we need to learn it is better to be in the fiery furnace *with* God than outside of the furnace *without* Him.

PRAYER: *Dear Lord, help me to trust You when my children walk through the fiery furnaces of life. I release them to Your care. Amen.*

DAY FIVE : JESUS DIED FOR YOUR FISH

READING: *Now I give him back to the Lord. He will belong to the Lord all his life* (1 Samuel 1:28 NCV).

OBSERVATION: One of these days, I should write a book about the funny things that have happened to me on the mission field. On a trip to Guadalajara, Mexico, one of our team members asked to address the crowd in Spanish. I thought, "Why not?"

As she spoke, laughter began to fill the town square. Since my Spanish is limited, I did not know if she had turned into a Hispanic comedienne, or if something else was going on. As the laughter grew louder, someone told me she had confused the Spanish words for "fish" (*pescado*) and "sin" (*pecado*). She was telling the people, "Jesus died to save you from your fish." Then, quoting that great passage in the book of Romans, she said, "For all have fished and come short of the glory of God." Finally she said, "If you will lay your 'fish' at the feet of Jesus, He will take it and bury it in the deepest sea." In spite of the Spanish slipups, the Holy Spirit moved mightily, and many people came to know Jesus as their Savior.

Young people make a difference in the kingdom of God. However, many student missions organizations, including Awe Star, reported a significant decrease in the number of participants after 9/11. This is disturbing news, because youth are a dynamic resource in the kingdom of God. Why?

1. *They have time.* Doing missions requires two things: time and resources. Most youth have the time, but they need some help with the resources. When both elements come together, the world had better . . . watch out!

2. *They are young.* In some countries, two-thirds of the population is under the age of fifteen. Youth effectively reach . . . youth.

3. *They are flexible.* They have a "can do" attitude. For young people, sleeping on the ground, riding in the backs of Jeeps, and enduring other inconveniences all make the experience more exciting.

4. *They are not afraid.* Young people possess a rare boldness and often, a desire for the extreme—even in reaching out to others.

5. *They need a rite of passage event.* In a generation where young people are not given significant tasks, missions activities move them from adolescence into adulthood.

God uses youth to make His name known. He may be speaking to your child or grandchild's heart right now, moving him or her to take a step toward a short-term missions experience. Talk, pray, encourage, and above all . . . allow them to go. Your children have something the whole world needs.

Besides, if your child fails to go, who will tell a lost world that Jesus will save them from their . . . fish?

PRINCIPLE: Early on, plant in your children's minds that that they are called to be "salt and light" in today's world.

PRAYER: *Dear Father, I want my children to see their purpose through Your eyes. They have been wonderfully made to become reflectors of Your glory. I would be honored if You would call them to be Your ambassadors in places where very few have gone. Thank You for trusting me with these children. Amen.*

〜

LOGICAL CONSEQUENCES

GOALS, SESSION FOUR:

1. Learners will understand and identify the need to provide children with *logical consequences* (predictable outcomes of an action).
2. Learners will begin to embrace the idea that, as good parents who seek the "ancient paths," they will want to provide logical consequences for their children.
3. Learners will begin to develop logical consequences contracts to use with their children in various areas of their own family life.

FACILITATORS: Before this session, please visit www.ropparenting.com and download the Session Four ROPPcast. This vidcast contains the *How It Shows* Bible teaching with Walker Moore to use later in the session.

MAKE YOURSELF AT HOME

I'm sure you understand by now why I refer to my younger son, Caleb, as my "special child." Another noteworthy episode in his young life became a perfect illustration of the third Essential Experience emphasized in ROPP.

It all began with a call I received from the principal of Caleb's school. Now, I was used to getting

FACILITATORS: As the group gathers, encourage members to begin reviewing the questions from the 51% Homework in Session Three (p. 90). You may prefer to work through these in reverse order so you can save the sharing about specific significant tasks for the end of the discussion. When nearly everyone is present, stop and pray together. Affirm members by reminding them that they are good parents who have now completed half the sessions and more than half of the *ROPP* material!

As we progress through this workbook, the questions become more practical . . . and personal. This adds to the learning opportunities . . . and the potential level of discomfort. Make sure to share your own struggles as well as successes, and avoid wounding anyone who reveals a point of vulnerability.

calls from Caleb's principal. It all began on his first day of kindergarten—but that's another story. This time, the principal's request seemed simple enough: Caleb had forgotten his lunch. Since the school had not been able to reach Cathy, he wanted me to retrieve the missing meal and bring it to my son before his lunch period.

I had just one question: why? Why should I spend time and gas to cover my son's mistake? Why couldn't we allow him to experience the *logical consequences* of forgetting his lunch?

After all, our family practiced logical consequences all the time. If you didn't get up in time, you missed breakfast. If you didn't do your homework, you couldn't watch television. It worked at home, so why not at school? I wanted to take a few minutes to explain our family system—and talk to the principal about how we could work together to extend Caleb's education—but for some reason, he hung up on me when I had barely begun my presentation.

I'm like most guys. The phrase "out of sight, out of mind" applies to me most of the time. In this case, once I got off the phone, I forgot all about my hungry son. If I *had* thought about Caleb and his lunch situation, I would have assumed that he would use his natural creative abilities. He would wheel and deal and put together a much more interesting meal than the one sitting at home on our kitchen counter.

Caleb never had the chance, as I found out a couple of days later when I received an unexpected bill from the school district for (you guessed it) one hot lunch. When I failed to agree immediately to the principal's request, he assumed he needed to cover for me . . . and for my son. The school district, like our society in general, wanted to protect Caleb from the logical consequences of his mistake. "Even if they *had* insisted on feeding him," I thought as I stuffed the bill back into its envelope, "they could have at least let him work off the cost of the meal. Hey— maybe that's what I can do now. . . "

We've all had those times where someone covered for the logical consequences we should have experienced. Can you think of a time in your life where this occurred? Maybe the police officer gave you a warning instead of the traffic ticket you deserved. Maybe your teacher looked the other way when you turned in an assignment two days late. In the space below, record at least one incident in which you missed a logical consequence that you deserved.

 ROPP TERMS:

LOGICAL CONSEQUENCES: The predictable outcomes of an action.

DADSPEAK: *Life in a rural community seems to center around rainfall. It seemed we were always waiting for rain, complaining because we had too much rain, or comparing this year's rainfall to last year's. My dad owned a progression of rain gauges throughout his life. He could tell you, down to a sixteenth of an inch, exactly how much rain we had three days—or even three years—ago.*

One Christmas, my brothers and I bought him the perfect present: a brand-new rain gauge. I suppose the gauges they sell today are analog, digital, and carry their own GPS units. Back then, this "deluxe" model had a large glass receptacle, bright-red measurement markings, and a beautiful picture of a rain cloud on one side. My little chest swelled with pride as Dad unwrapped it and looked at it from every angle. As soon as we finished the rush of opening presents, he went outside, walking down our long driveway so he could mount his prized possession in just the right spot.

That year, I had a new Christmas present to try out too. On the farm, a boy knew he was growing up when he got his own BB gun. Now, it was my turn. Once I tore the package open, I could hardly wait to get outside.

After Dad had gone outside with his present, I made my way out with mine. I stood on the porch, held up the BB gun, and looked through its sight. I was impressed. I could see almost all the way down the gravel drive. I could even see Dad, hands on his hips, admiring the new rain gauge. I drew a bead and pretended to pull the trigger. Wouldn't it be great to have such good aim that I could actually hit something so small and distant as the glass barrel of that gauge?

You can guess what happened. My "pretend" trigger-pull accidentally became reality. My dad's prize present exploded right in front of him, and he jumped back as if fire had fallen from heaven. I couldn't read his expression, but I watched in horror as he stared at the remnants of his beautiful new rain gauge, now shattered at his feet.

The few moments it took him to return to the porch were some of the longest hours of my life. I stood frozen, awaiting the inevitable. After all, I was right there on the porch. I had the new BB gun. He knew I had committed the crime, and things would only get worse if I tried to deny my guilt. "I'm sorry, I'm sorry, I'm sorry," I stammered, tears streaming down my face.

Dad's big work boots clumped across the porch. He

didn't even look at me as he passed. He didn't say anything, either—and that made things seem even worse. I lived with the guilt of destroying his present for a very long time. Dad never said a single word about it.

If he had only followed his usual pattern of spanking me or disciplining me in some other way, I would have considered the sin forgiven and the case closed. Deep in their hearts, children know, expect, and desire logical consequences. When they don't receive them—especially when they rarely or never receive them—it's . . . wrong.

WHAT'S MISSING?

Not only are logical consequences becoming increasingly rare in our culture, but we also tend to remove their *logic* as often as we can. In fact, our kids rarely experience predictable outcomes of any kind, because we don't allow them to occur. Parents who *do* give logical consequences, in fact, are often labeled "bad" parents. Think about it: a sixth-grade boy comes to school soaking wet because he forgot his raincoat. Wouldn't the school assume his parents were to blame? What about the third-grader who misses the first few minutes of soccer practice because she didn't complete her homework on time? Would the coach be upset with the child for not finishing the homework, or with the "mean" mother who kept her home?

Sometimes God uses logical consequences to teach important lessons. If we place our hands on a hot stove, we will get burned. If we don't get enough sleep, we will feel tired. Do you remember a logical consequence you experienced as a child that taught you a lesson? Write the logical consequence and a one-sentence summary of its accompanying lesson on the following page.

ROPP: And yet, I guarantee that going against the mainstream and putting logical consequences back into your kids' lives is one of the best things you will ever do for them. The logical consequences they experience now will instill qualities in them that will help them grow into capable, responsible, self-reliant adults. In other words, logical consequences help Rite of Passage Parents equip their kids . . . for life. *(Rite of Passage Parenting)*

When I was growing up in Missouri, I lived, except for a short time, in a rural area that supported logical consequences. Members of this Irish community all supported the *same* logical consequences for the *same* offenses because we shared the *same* values and beliefs. We even had a rule: any parent could spank any child. Our country was settled in communities like this made of people who shared the same beliefs and values, often because of a common heritage or religious background. In these small pockets, everyone knew how to identify right from wrong because values and beliefs were so similar.

However, as our culture shifted and families began moving away from the farm, these communities shifted too. Norwegians, like my beautiful wife's family, moved from Wisconsin to Missouri, bringing their values and beliefs along with them. Some of the Irish in Missouri headed for Chicago, and other cultural groups with their own values and beliefs split up, moved around, and mixed with others to produce . . . the cultural chaos we have today.

That's one more reason ROPP emphasizes a return to the ancient paths laid down before the foundations of time. When we go back to what God says, our values and beliefs won't be mixed up. We won't have a clash of cultures or communities. We'll define right and wrong based on His will and Word, and we'll get back to His way of producing capable, responsible, self-reliant adults. Those are the kinds of logical consequences I . . . love.

⚡ CULTURE SHOCK: An Ohio mother who was fed up with her family not picking up their things went to extremes to clean house, Cleveland television station WEWS reported.

Jessica Schickel created a box filled with all the items that were not put in their proper place and sold them on eBay.

The winning bidder got all the items and a videotape of the family's reaction when they found out their possessions were sold behind their backs.

Schickel said she just had a baby and was fed up with her other two children and her husband not picking up their belongings.

The box of prized possessions sold for over $300. But Schickel said her family still hasn't gotten the message.

"They didn't learn their lesson, so it's their own fault," said Schickel.

Schickel has started collecting items for a second box. All proceeds earned will be donated to charity.[1]

⚡ CULTURE SHOCK: A school in New York has adopted a policy that sends parents to detention if they show up late to drop off their children.

The New York Post reported that the Manhattan School for Children, an elite public school that has been nationally recognized, adopted the new rule in order to motivate parents to deliver their children to school on time in the mornings.

👤 FACILITATORS: Take some time here to read and discuss the two "Culture Shock" articles with your group. Adapt the questions that follow as appropriate for your group dynamics.

ROPP Terms:

VALUES: The things that an individual deems worthy or prizes.

BELIEFS: Thoughts expressed as actions.

CHARACTER: Moral core that defines an individual's identity.

Under the policy, tardy parents must pick up a late slip in the office and then go to the auditorium for a 20-minute time out.

The new policy was announced in a letter to parents last summer. Still, as many as five parents a day have reportedly been sent into detention, the *Post* said.

Some parents denounce the rule as silly and going too far, the report said. Others believe in it, saying it's a real source of morning motivation.[2]

What do you think? Both of these articles clearly point to a cultural shift—but what do you think about the consequences mentioned in each one? Are they logical? Write an L beside the article if you think the consequences fit the situation, and prepare to discuss with your spouse or group.

BUILDING PROJECT

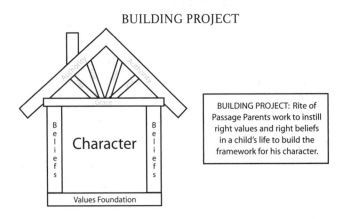

BUILDING PROJECT: Rite of Passage Parents work to instill right values and right beliefs in a child's life to build the framework for his character.

When I talk to parents about what's missing in kids' lives today, I like to use the analogy of a building project. God is the Architect and Builder, but as the parents, you take the role of the contractor. That means you need to lay a foundation made of right *values* overlaid by right *beliefs*. These two components combine to build the framework for your child's *character*. When the foundation and walls don't line up, cracks appear, and ultimately, the building is in danger of collapse.

How It Shows

ropp By the Numbers:

65 . . . percentage of underage youth who report that they get alcohol from family and friends with or without their permission.

31 . . . percentage of 15- to 20-year old drivers killed in fatal crashes in 2003 who had been drinking alcohol.[3]

55 . . . percentage increase of credit card debt of 25- to 34-year-olds from 1992 to 2001.[4]

14 . . . percentage of college students whose parents help them settle their credit card debts.[5]

Use the following blanks to fill in your own truth statements. If you're participating in this as part of a group setting, you will be asked to share your truth to avoid paying some not-so-logical consequences.

Tell the truth about the following:

• *A false rite of passage you took on before you became an adult.*

FACILITATORS: This section covers a great deal of material! For this reason, you may choose to spend more time on one section or question than another to ensure adequate understanding. You may also choose, if the group agrees, to break up this session and study it in two separate group times. Do your best as a sensitive leader to make sure that group members genuinely understand the material and to pray with and for them about taking the next step of applying it to their own family.

FACILITATORS: If time allows, read and briefly discuss these ropp By the Numbers statistics before proceeding to the following game, similar to the classic television show "Truth or Consequences". Ask participants to prepare by writing the truth statements in their books as explained below. For a group setting, use the statements as the basis for a game. Ask members to share their responses one at a time, using consequences that the group agrees upon if someone declines to share an answer.

Before this session, compile a short list of humorous consequences to use with the group (Example: drink a full glass of water nonstop, then crow like a rooster three times). Remember that you are still responsible to let your group members know that they are good parents, and encourage them by modeling honest, humble, and caring communication. Do not allow them to measure out any consequences that you would not willingly endure yourself!

• *A time when you acted like a helicopter parent.*

• *A simulator task you can't teach your kids because you don't know how to do it yourself.*

• *One logical consequence you'd like to give if you could (for example: sentence your mate to laundry duty for a month the next time he leaves his dirty clothes on the bedroom floor).*

• *Two logical or not-so-logical consequences you've handed out to your kids. If your children are too young or not yet born, you may list some that were given to you as a child (for example: you kept interrupting your mother, so she stuffed a sock into your mouth).*

It all began in the Garden—at least that's what Scripture says. When the Evil One wanted to attack God's ancient paths, he did it through the woman. He placed the plump, softly gleaming fruit at just the right angle to appeal to her sense of beauty. He gently pushed its delicate scent in her direction. Before long, he was whispering in a soft, understanding tone, "Did God *really* say . . .?" (Genesis 3:1 NCV).

As soon as he caused her to think twice, he had her. What *had* God said, anyway? The ancient path of obedience and trust in authority was broken right there. That was the moment when all who came after Eve began to question those in authority, to wonder . . . "Did he really say . . . ?"

Eve pondered—but only for a moment. Curiosity gave way to greed, and greed gave way to action. Within a few moments, she had removed the fruit from the tree, offered it to her partner, and taken those first condemning bites.

Nothing ever tasted so sweet. Nothing ever had such a bitter aftertaste. The guilty pair heard the footsteps, then the voice . . . of God. Always before, they had loved listening to Him speak. Today, as they wandered farther and farther from the ancient path, His words sounded harsh and angry in their guilty ears: "I've told you! If I've told you once, I told you a thousand times! How many times have I told you? *Don't eat the fruit of the tree of the knowledge of good and evil!"*

You probably know that God didn't berate His disobedient children in the way described here—the way that today's parents seem to have a hard time avoiding. Instead, He administered the logical consequences He had set up beforehand: you eat, you die. Adam and Eve ate, so they died—spiritually and

FACILITATORS: Facilitators who downloaded it will want to play the Bible teaching segment of the Session Four ROPPcast here. Whether or not you use this option, please go over the Bible teaching in the next few paragraphs and prepare to explain or read alongside your group and/or partner.

(ultimately) physically as well. They experienced the logical consequences of their actions, and they left the Garden, sadder and at least a little wiser.

You've seen it over and over: in the parenting world, times have changed! Parents today are far more inclined either to ignore or to lecture children about bad behavior than to allow them to experience logical consequences.

Think for a moment about a childish action that today's parents generally overlook but which your parents would not allow. Write it down here. If you received any type of consequence for this action, write it down as well. (For example, when I wiggled or whispered in the pew at church, my dad thumped me on the back of the head. One good thump was all it took to keep me quiet through an entire service.)

Let's return for a moment to the building project analogy. Remember that, as a parent, God has designated you as your child's character contractor. You're charged with supervising the subcontractors so the building will stand straight and true. Today, with multiple subcontractors holding multiple values, beliefs, and avenues of input into your child's life, you have a much harder job than parents did prior to the cultural shift. As our values-based communities began to disintegrate, the force of shared values and shared logical consequences began disintegrating also. Like many other ancient paths, the parental role of authority is often . . . forgotten.

The building project analogy also provides a good way to explain why even good parents like you and like me have so much trouble raising our kids. Even if we lay a foundation of right values—the ones based on the will and the Word of God—our culture adds wrong beliefs. If we fail to add logical consequences (and sometimes even when we do), the culture sends in more wrong beliefs. Even worse, today's mixed-up culture helps support these misplaced beliefs and values with *props* of false thinking. That also explains why the parent-contractors have to stay on the job 24/7, constantly supporting or fixing areas that fail to meet code.

The use of props to justify wrong behavior also explains the disconnect between what parents teach and the way kids act. For example, Mom and Dad teach Little Johnny to value good grades. However, little Johnny spends lots of time at school every day. His playground buddies introduce him to a wrong belief: it's okay to cheat on tests. Since little Johnny's newly adopted wrong belief won't match up with his right value, he supports it with a prop that says good grades are the surest way to a secure future—regardless of how he obtains them. When the prop falls, as it inevitably does, Little Johnny's building—and his character—are certain to collapse.

ROPP: We don't want to hurt our kids' feelings, so we allow them to watch a popular television show that has sexual overtones. We don't want to damage their self-esteem, so we buy them a toy every time we visit the store. We fear being accused of abuse, so we hesitate to discipline them. We don't even like to say, "No." After all, we're supposed to keep them happy . . . aren't we? *(Rite of Passage Parenting)*

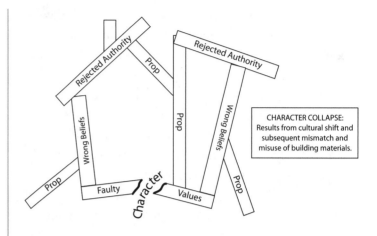

CHARACTER COLLAPSE:
Results from cultural shift and
subsequent mismatch and
misuse of building materials.

Use the space here to give an example of a right value matched with a wrong belief that you see in your family or in our culture in general. For example: a high school student values her sexuality (right value), so she decides to wait to have intercourse until a boyfriend says that he "loves" her (wrong belief).

ROPP TERMS:

PROPS: Statements of false thinking or faulty logic used to justify wrong beliefs or wrong values.

VALUABLE: Deemed worthy, prized.

NON-VALUABLE: Deemed non-worthy or unimportant.

An important aspect of Rite of Passage Parenting is teaching kids to make wise choices that will build healthy lives. Properly applied logical consequences can equip kids for life by teaching them the difference between *valuable* and *non-valuable*. Today, few kids experience the logical consequences of poor (non-valuable) choices, so they fail to understand the real dangers that can come their way. We look at their actions and shake our heads, wondering, "What were you *thinking?*"

I have noticed four main areas in which the Enemy is working hard to gain control of our kids' lives—generally by means of *valuable* and *non-valuable* choices. The first area, *language,* affects even very young children. A glance at almost any television show or movie reveals this result of the cultural shift. Language that used to be considered profane (non-valuable) has become a part of everyday speech. Kids come home from school, church, or sports activities repeating words that their parents may not have understood until much later in life.

The area of *possessions* represents another area of concern. Kids today have way too much—and we keep giving them more. It's not uncommon for elementary school children to have their own cell phones, computers, and the latest video game consoles equipped with multiple game choices. One thing, however, hasn't changed: kids' belongings still end up scattered across the floor or left at a friend's house. Do they know the difference between valuable and non-valuable possessions? I don't think so.

Closely tied to the area of *possessions* is that of *finances.* As I travel across the country, I see more and more evidence of the *spirit of entitlement* that says, "because I exist, therefore you owe me" certain things . . . including money. College students expect parents to pick up the tab not only for their education, but for their cell phone, fast-food cravings, automobile insurance, and other bills. If they run out of money, a quick phone call to mom and dad solves everything . . . at least, they think it does. Capable, responsible, self-reliant adults have learned how to manage their finances. In today's society, that's increasingly . . . rare.

The final area will not surprise anyone in touch

ROPP TERMS:

SPIRIT OF
ENTITLEMENT: An
individual's belief that he
is owed money, time,
possessions, etc. as a
function of mere existence:
"I am; therefore you owe
me."

INNOCENCE: Purity in
mind, body, soul, and
spirit.

LOSS OF INNOCENCE:
Corruption of one or more
aspects of purity in mind,
body, soul, or spirit.

with the news. Our world is exploding with the impact of a heightened emphasis on *sexuality*. As the culture, through multiple media inputs, sends sexual messages to younger and younger kids, they move away from the ancient path God has designed. At birth, He gives everyone a gift to share with just one other person: the gift of *innocence*. The Enemy wants to steal this precious gift by making sexuality appear non-valuable. Now, even very young children acquire what in the past was adult knowledge, causing an early and painful *loss of innocence*. The high price of this loss, a burden of guilt from poor choices, can negatively affect the individual and his or her marriage for years to come.

Sometimes, it's scary to be a parent—especially a good one who cares about your kids. The impact of the cultural shift on these four areas (language, possessions, finances, and sexuality) affects almost every family. Write here the area that, as a parent, scares you the most—and, if you're part of a group, be prepared to share why.

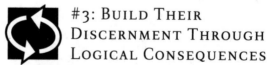 #3: BUILD THEIR
DISCERNMENT THROUGH
LOGICAL CONSEQUENCES

Properly applied logical consequences, such as allowing Little Johnny to fail a test after a teacher catches him cheating, help match right values to right beliefs and prepare him for responsible living. That's why I like to say *Where there are no logical consequences, there are no values.* Teaching one without applying the other results in the mixed-up, messed-up, irresponsible lives that we often see today.

This coincides with another saying, the one I told you that I like to share with parents as I speak across the country: *you can pay now, or pay later.* Properly applying logical consequences will cost you time and effort. However, the cost of *not* applying them is much higher. Even if your children are older—even much older—it's not too late. At any time, you can go back, put logical consequences back into their lives, and begin to rebuild. Make the wise decision to pay now . . . so you and your family can avoid paying later.

Whether or not you've had the opportunity to apply logical consequences in your own parenting, chances are that you know someone who has. Use this space to jot down a few notes about someone you know who has effectively used logical consequences to discipline his or her children. What have you seen, and how has it worked?

FACILITATORS: The following questions are deliberately designed to help parents begin to consider the ways God can use the ROPP principles in their own lives. Please know that this session may begin addressing areas of pain or stress. I suggest that group leaders model personal application by sharing an experience of your own before asking for members' input. Your honesty and openness count for much more than your skill in carrying out the logical consequences. Remember . . . *you're* a good parent too!

How can Rite of Passage Parents find a practical way of communicating their values? First, look to the ancient paths. How did God communicate His values? He developed contracts.

ROPP: The Bible is the written record of His contract with us; in fact the word *testament* means "contract." We have an old contract (Old Testament) and a new contract (New Testament). In the Bible, God explains things very clearly: if you don't do this, this is what will happen. From the very beginning, God always communicated clearly. Remember? "[If you eat] of the tree . . . you shall surely die" (Genesis 2:17). . . . When we contract with our children, we are giving them a written record of our values. (*Rite of Passage Parenting*)

I recommend that you gradually begin to develop logical consequences contracts with your children. Each will teach a value or belief, along with a list of specific things you want them to do—like hang up their clothes and dust the furniture in their room—or not do—like leave their toys scattered across the floor. Logical consequences contracting takes the emotion out of values instruction. It also prevents parental stresses like constantly reminding ("Clean your room. Clean your room. Aren't you listening? I said, CLEAN YOUR ROOM!"); giving in and doing the work for the child; or ignoring the problem until it gets so bad that an emotional and/or verbal explosion occurs. I recommend that you work on just one contract at a time: Write it out, sign it, and then post it on that most sacred family message center: the refrigerator door.

ROPP *describes Logical Consequences Contracts for four key areas: language, possessions, finances, and sexuality. Which area do you see as the biggest need in your own family, and why? Write your answer below.*

The Fix-Its at the end of this session give specific examples of logical consequences contracts, but before you check those, let's examine ways to deal with the four problem areas mentioned above. First, I recommend that parents and kids develop *language contracts*. When my oldest son came home from kindergarten with a *very* bad expression that he innocently shared with his Bible-thumping great-grandmother, I knew I had to do something . . . and fast. Jeremiah and I began to work on the contract we called the Good Word/Bad Word Project.

God's ancient paths are . . . good. I told my sons that Satan takes what is good and tries to make it bad—so we now have "bad" words for things that God has already deemed "good." Our contract was simple: Jeremiah could say any of the new words he learned at school—to his mom and me, when we discussed it during our evening family time. At that point, he could decide whether it belonged on the "good" or "bad" side of a chart we began making together, and use or avoid it accordingly.

The discussions we had with our boys about good and bad words for bodily functions, anatomy, and sexuality formed the foundation for the more advanced discussions we had as they matured. At very young ages, they learned to use correct terminology rather than rude slang. We also witnessed an unexpected benefit. Through a process called "transference of learning," the boys began assigning "good" or "bad" values to almost everything they encountered. I considered this . . . invaluable.

We all have areas of parenting that we find more or less comfortable. On a scale of 1–10 (1 low and 10 high), rate how comfortable you are with the idea of using a language contract like this with your family.

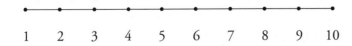

1   2   3   4   5   6   7   8   9   10

The next logical consequences contract addresses a nearly universal parenting problem: getting kids to clean up their bedrooms. Before I teach you about the contract, let me point out a communication mistake that parents make without even realizing it. When we speak to our kids, moms and dads often use *adultisms*. These, according to educator Stephen Glenn, "occur any time an adult forgets what it is like to be a child and then expects, demands, and requires of the child, who has never been an adult, to think, act, understand, see, and do things as an adult."[6]

When you develop a logical consequences *possessions contract*, you need to lay things out step by step. If you simply say "clean the room," he will generally do it . . . according to his standards. However, if you write out exactly what you mean (see example in Fix-It #4-1, page 130) by "clean the room," he will have a much more specific guide to follow, and a much better chance of ending up with the kind of room you like.

We gave a unique consequence as a part of our possessions contracts. I told my boys that when they left their belongings scattered around, they were deeming them non-valuable. Our contract allowed us to do a sweep of the house or bedroom. We could take any belongings our sons left lying around to a particular store, such as Goodwill, that restores value to these non-valuable items. Just one or two donations to that special store helped the boys realize that fulfilling their possessions contract was . . . valuable.

There's no doubt about it. We've all used adultisms with our kids. List on the following page one or more that you've said yourself—or that you remember your parents using as they spoke to you.

FACILITATORS: The concept of adultisms may be somewhat difficult to grasp, but once parents "get it," they'll be able to stop the damage they cause by using them. Discussing the next question will help, especially if you prepare your own examples of adultisms ahead of time. An additional list is available in the Session Four Facilitator's Helps at www.ropparenting.com.

MOMSPEAK: *Logical consequences is an area of ROPP that really hit . . . home. Although Tom and I had built consequences into our kids' lives, they weren't always logical, and they didn't always follow the consistent pattern of ROPP. Walker's teaching helped me to understand that I found logical consequences difficult because, like many moms, I'm more comfortable with grace than law. Moms like me often find it easier to pick up after our kids or do their forgotten chores than to remind them constantly or face the messes they left behind. When I followed this pattern, though, guess who experienced the logical consequences? You're right—no one else but me. I felt frustrated, angry, and upset. I never sold their belongings on eBay—but I sometimes thought about putting my kids up for sale!*

ROPP's emphasis on logical consequences has freed me from taking on my kids' tasks. If they don't complete a chore, I don't have to nag or get upset. I simply check the logical consequences and deliver them—at least 51 percent of the time. Because my children know about the consequences in advance, the choice to experience them is just that: their choice. As they continue to mature, they enjoy negotiating with Tom and me about which logical consequences they experience. Allowing them to express their opinions takes away some of the sting of the discipline when it occurs. All of this has brought incredible freedom to my parenting, especially now that I realize that these logical consequences build toward our goal of building responsibility into our kids' lives.

The *finances contract* tackles some of the problems arising from our culture's emphasis on bigger, better, and more, more, more. Cathy and I regularly used this type of contract to help our boys learn money management. Each season, we would determine their needs for new clothing and budget a sufficient amount to cover each item. The boys could then take that amount and use it to meet the need as they chose. If they chose wisely and watched for sale items, they could keep any extra funds for themselves. If they chose unwisely or lost an item they had purchased (as Jeremiah did one year when he left his coat at school), Cathy and I would not buy a replacement until the term of that contract was complete.

The finances contracts went a long way toward teaching our sons to manage their money. Caleb has recently experienced extra blessings through his faithful adherence to principles he learned as a young boy. Jeremiah (who, during the winter of the lost coat, ended up wearing one bought with his own money at that special Goodwill store) graduated from college completely debt-free—a lifestyle he and his wife maintain today.

♥ WHAT ARE THE ODDS? I'm a husband and father. I'm a pastor. I'm also a musician—a trumpet player. My horn-playing helped me understand and apply logical consequences in my kids' lives even before I learned about Walker's ROPP principles.

Musicians like me experience logical consequences every day. If I practice, I play better. The notes come out clearer and stronger. If I don't practice for a few days, the notes are less predictable and consistent, my tone thins out, and I have to work a lot harder to give the appearance of a decent effort.

When I haven't been practicing, my endurance disappears. The muscles that support my playing retain the memory to do their job, but they lose their stamina very quickly. Within just a few minutes, I've lost all the strength to do what I have to do. When this happens, I suffer, and you can bet that my music suffers. Oh, I can fake it temporarily—but only temporarily.

I tell my trumpet students they can *pay now or pay later* (Walker and I think a lot alike). If you *pay now* by taking time to practice, your playing improves. If you don't practice, your playing suffers—you *pay later.* Those simple logical consequences have kept me practicing my horn on a fairly consistent basis for all but the first nine years of my life!

This explains why my wife and I work hard to design consequences for our kids to match areas of their lives that need attention. I make choices about my practicing based on the logical consequences I've experienced. In the same way, properly applied logical consequences motivate our kids to make wise choices—to do the right thing.

I don't want to shield my kids from an ancient path that will help them build right values for right living. As far as I'm concerned, logical consequences are music to my ears.—Tom Pieper[7]

The final logical consequences contract, dealing with the area of *sexuality,* is the one you'd probably prefer to avoid. Let me ask you just one question: do you want to pay now, or pay later? Regardless of how uncomfortable you feel, the costs of not dealing with this crucial area are high—for you, and especially for your child.

In some ways, however, the sexuality contract is easier on mom and dad than any of the others. In this area in particular, young people must make their own choices. That, and the fact that studies show that those who date in their early teens are much more likely to become sexually involved,[8] is why I recommend that you not allow your child to date until he has completed his rite of passage event, is at least sixteen years old, and has developed his own contract for sexuality.

Work on other logical consequences contracts first. Make them a regular practice in your family life. Discuss the following chart of sexual activity with your kids (if you are unfamiliar with some of the specific terms, see the Rite of Passage Parenting Glossary and/or Chapter 9 in *Rite of Passage Parenting).* By the time your children begin to reach physical maturity, they can take the principles you have taught and apply them to this area of their lives as well.

The process of negotiating logical consequences contracts empowers and enables young people to make wise choices based on right values and right beliefs. It's one of the healthiest ways I know to begin equipping your kids . . . for life.

ASSIGNING VALUES TO SEXUALITY

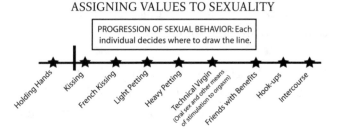

PROGRESSION OF SEXUAL BEHAVIOR: Each individual decides where to draw the line.

Holding Hands | Kissing | French Kissing | Light Petting | Heavy Petting | Technical Virgin (Oral sex and other means of stimulation to orgasm) | Friends with Benefits | Hook-ups | Intercourse

Even for a good parent like you, the idea of tying logical consequences to behaviors as a method of training and instruction may be new. Think about your own family and some of the areas where you have ongoing conflicts. Could the application of logical consequences help you? Go back to the areas of need you listed on page 122. As time allows, work on your own or as a group to determine a logical consequence that might help you "fix it."

 51 PERCENT: This week, concentrate on the following *ROPP* handles:

1. Writing logical consequences contracts is an important element of ROPP. Look at the sample contracts in the Fix-Its at the end of this session. Choose one area for which you would like to develop a contract. Follow the basic plan and write out the area, the actions, and the logical consequences that will result. Go over this with your spouse to make any additions or corrections. DO NOT TRY THIS AT HOME . . . YET. You need the essential information you'll learn in our next session (Grace Deposits) before you're ready to properly and completely apply your learning.

2. If you have the opportunity, read and/or review Section Four, "Essential Element #4: Grace Deposits," in *ROPP* (Chapters 10–12).

3. Over a five-day period before beginning the next session, read and study the five-day ROPP Devotion Guide that follows the Fix-Its for this chapter. Next, complete the following: *Which devotion did the most "rearranging" in your heart this week? Write the day/title below, along with a few words about why you found it especially meaningful.*

Fix-It #4-1:
Possessions Contract for a Clean Room

PRINCIPLE: *Valuable* versus *non-valuable*

SCRIPTURE: *Honor the LORD with your possessions, And with the firstfruits of all your increase* (Proverbs 3:9).

SUMMARY: We assign values to everything in life. For instance, if I gave you a used Kleenex, you would probably tell me it wasn't valuable—that it should be thrown away. If I gave you a hundred-dollar bill, you would probably tell me that it was worth a lot of money. Would you throw this $100 away along with the used Kleenex? No!

Some things are more valuable than others. We take care of valuable things. Non-valuable things can be thrown away—but something even better occurs if we can give them value by redeeming them. Many people recycle non-valuable items, and others take this trash and redeem it by turning it into something that has value once again.

SURRENDER: I understand the difference between valuable and non-valuable. Anything that my parents find scattered on my bedroom floor, I have deemed non-valuable. Since I have deemed it non-valuable, I want to be a good steward and make it valuable again. That is what God did on the cross: He redeemed us and made us valuable again.

THEREFORE, any items left scattered on the bedroom floor will be taken to Goodwill so that those who are less fortunate can receive the blessing of non-valuable items made valuable again.

Child/date

_____

_____

Mom and Dad/date

_____

_____

FIX-IT #4-2:
FINANCES CONTRACT FOR CLOTHING

PRINCIPLE: *Wants* versus *Needs*

SCRIPTURE: *And having food and clothing, with these we shall be content* (1 Timothy 6:8).

SUMMARY: As your parents, God has charged us with the responsibility of meeting your basic needs, including food to eat and clothes to wear. We acknowledge our responsibility to provide these things, as well as to prepare you to assume full responsibility for them one day. Although we often provide things you *want*, our true responsibility lies in providing what you *need*.

As a part of meeting your need for clothing, we will supply you with three good pairs of jeans for the school year. We have learned that you can purchase quality jeans for around $20 a pair. For this school year, we will give you a $60 jeans allowance. If you want to spend $50 on a pair of designer jeans, you will only be able to buy one pair, and you will have to wear them until the time of the next clothing allowance. If you choose to buy jeans that are less expensive than $20 a pair, you may keep the extra money to spend as you wish.

SURRENDER: I understand that the responsibility for buying my school jeans is now mine. I understand that my parents have allotted me a specific amount of money to purchase my basic needs. I understand that I will have to live with the decisions I make until the time of the next clothing allowance. I accept the responsibility of making decisions for my clothing.

Child/date

_____

_____

Mom and Dad/date

_____

_____

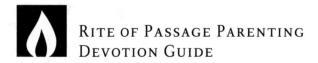

RITE OF PASSAGE PARENTING
DEVOTION GUIDE

DAY ONE: HANGING ON . . . AND ON

READING: *"But if you fail to do this, you will be sinning against the LORD; and you may be sure that your sin will find you out"* (Numbers 32:23 NIV).

OBSERVATION: Where do coat hangers come from? How do they multiply?

I don't know the answer to either question! Years ago, when I moved out of my parents' home, my mom gave me two coat hangers and some other necessities.

A few days later, something mysterious had happened: I now owned four hangers. Before I knew it, I was hauling coat hangers out of my closet by the grocery sack-loads. This phenomenon continues today.

I have tried everything to stop their propagation. First, I tried separating the males from the females, but I was never sure which was which. You can find anything you need on the Internet, but when I typed in "coat hanger population control," I found . . . nothing.

I am not even sure exactly when the multiplication process occurs. I tried leaving my closet light on to discourage their nighttime activity, but nothing seems to work. Even worse, some of my neighbor's hangers have now migrated to my closet. I have fat hangers, skinny hangers, metal hangers, plastic hangers, crocheted-covered hangers, brown, green, wooden, and even chrome hangers. Because I travel internationally, my hanger collection represents every country of the world.

I have tried giving them away and even putting them out to be recycled. Unfortunately, hangers are like the dog left behind when its owners moved away. Somehow, they always manage to find their way home. Besides, if you give away one hanger . . . you get back two.

Character faults are the only things that multiply faster than coat hangers. That reminds me of a story . . . Some children found a lion cub in the jungle. The village chief became very upset and said, "Little lion grows up to become big lion, and big lion kills."

No one would listen to the chief because the cub looked so innocent. But the little lion did grow up, and it killed the boy who found it.

Parents: help your children overcome character faults. Little lies grow up to become big lies, and big lies kill. It is much easier to deal with a child's character faults than an adult's. As I often say to parents: pay now, or you will pay later. Don't ignore little problems in hopes that they'll go away.

Now . . . if we could only find a way to kill those coat hangers!

PRINCIPLE: Your child's character faults today will be his downfall tomorrow.

PRAYER: *Dear Father, I know I have flaws that I wished my parents had helped me eliminate. What seemed harmless years ago now haunts me regularly. Please give me wisdom to correct my own character faults as I deal with my child. Thank You that we can lean on Your flawless character. Amen.*

DAY TWO: DRVTHRUSPKRS

READING: *When He had called the multitude to Himself, He said to them, "Hear and understand"* (Matthew 15:10).

OBSERVATION: What man can and cannot do . . . amuses me. Primitive man built the pyramids without using electricity or seeing a single episode of "This Old House." Modern man can make a satellite that can hover high above the earth, zoom down, and read your license plate, all while your vehicle is traveling at seventy miles an hour.

So far, however, man has not been able to develop an understandable speaker for the drive-through area of a fast food restaurant. As we get older, our hearing tends to wane, so I am getting to the point where I would rather order inside than go through the hassle of learning "speaker language." The other day, I pulled up to a popular fast food eatery, rolled down my window, and heard: "VelcometomezenhzwcanIhelpu?"

"Yes, I would like to order a double cheeseburger with fries and a Diet Coke."

The speaker sputtered, "Adblechezzeburgerfrize&dizecke?"

Now, I knew someone had just said something, but it always takes a minute for the sound to travel from my ear through the "translator" brain cells so I can understand. Finally, I realized that the speaker had simply repeated my order. I answered, "Yes."

The speaker sputtered again, "Wldulikit SUPER-SIZED?" (For some reason, the only two words that can be broadcast clearly are "super-sized.")

"No, thank you," I responded.

"Plzepulrndnxtwndow."

Relieved that I was about to speak to a real human being, I drove around the corner. The cashier opened the window and said, "Thzwillbethreeeghty." At that moment, I realized that the problem was not the speaker. Instead, it was *the speaker.*

Most teenagers believe that there is very little difference between their parents and the speakers used for drive-through windows. As parents, we make many sounds that teenagers translate as muffled murmurings. Sociologists call these phrases *adultisms,* in which a parent speaks to a child who has limited life experiences, expecting him or her to understand. This is why you must define for your child exactly what "clean your room" means. Does it mean "Make a path from the door to the closet"? Does it mean "Shove everything under the bed"? Or maybe "Make the bed, hang up all clothes, put all dirty clothes in the hamper, and dust all the furniture"?

Explanations define exactly what the speaker expects. Adultisms force the listener to assume he or she understands. The first produces confidence and clarity. The second produces anxiety . . . and often, rooms that no mother would define as "clean."

PRINCIPLE: Clear communication exists only when understanding is achieved.

PRAYER: *Dear Father, thank You for communicating Your love clearly through the cross. Today, may I be a clear communicator of Your truth to my children. I want them to hear and understand what a mighty God we serve. May my words reflect Your words, and may my thoughts be Your thoughts. Amen.*

DAY THREE: THE LAND OF SOMEWHERE

READING: *Your word I have hidden in my heart, that I might not sin against You* (Psalm 119:11).

OBSERVATION: Some of my most vivid childhood memories come from our many family vacations. You notice I didn't say "fond" memories . . . but "vivid" ones. Since we were poor, our vacations always consisted of camping out. I never knew we were poor. I just thought our family was adventurous, and the people who stayed in hotels were the poor ones who couldn't afford camping equipment. In fact, my parents judged each vacation according to its "roughing it" factor.

For instance, the farther away from civilization we got, the higher my parents ranked the vacation on the "roughing it" scale. If we woke up in the morning and our water bucket was frozen, the trip got extra points. Bears and other life-threatening animals crawling around outside gave it even more points. And if we had to spend the night holding our tent down during a Category Five hurricane, that vacation won the "roughing it" award, hands down. Every year, we would head out again, trying to see if we could outdo the previous year's vacation by standing face-to-face with danger and coming home to brag about it.

We took many pictures of these vacations. On the back of every photo, my parents would write "somewhere in Colorado," or "somewhere in Wyoming," or sometimes just "somewhere." Since our family was lost most of the time (of course, being lost gave the vacation extra points on the "roughing it" scale), we could never give you many details about where we had been. We just knew that we had gone "somewhere."

In our family, however, "somewhere" wasn't limited to vacations. "Somewhere" also had to do with Bible references. My parents would say, "Somewhere in the Bible it tells us that you shouldn't hit your little brother." "Somewhere in the Bible it says to clean your plate, make your bed, and wash behind your ears." I was never sure where the Bible said those things, but I knew it must say them "somewhere."

As a child, you have to accept the "somewheres," but as you get older, you begin to question them. You realize that "somewhere" isn't good enough. You don't want your eternity based on "somewhere," but on the truth—on a real knowledge of the Scriptures.

As parents, we need to give our children a place where they can go to *verify* the truth. "Somewhere" may make a nice vacation spot, but it comes with a big problem: you can never find your way back again.

Now, where are those vacation photos? I know I put them somewhere. . . .

PRINCIPLE: Teaching your children to hide God's Word in their hearts equips them for life.

PRAYER: *Father, I pledge that I will teach my children to hide Your Word in their hearts, and help me to do the same. I want our faith to stand on ground more solid than "somewhere."*

DAY FOUR: HOMESPUN WISDOM

READING: *Put on the whole armor of God, that you may be able to stand against the wiles of the devil* (Ephesians 6:11).

REFLECTION: I grew up with a mother who loved to read, and she instilled that same love in me. Mom did not read *War and Peace* or *The History of the World*, but she read the Bible, Christian books, newspapers, magazines, and *Capper's Weekly.*

If you do not remember *Capper's Weekly*, your education is incomplete. Reading it was as close as church-going folks could come to reading *The National Enquirer.* Everybody in the family read *Capper's Weekly.* Each issue contained devotional thoughts; a story of a brave soul who survived a blizzard or other natural disaster; and something disgusting, like a picture of the world's largest tomato worm. It also contained practical articles with tips for living like "How to Get Your Plants Adjusted to Daylight-Saving Time" or "Ten Ways to Get Beet Juice Out of Your Apron."

Capper's Weekly was entertaining and useful. Recently, I was thinking about submitting some of my helpful hints for its editors to consider.

1. If you are submitting a resumé for a job with UPS, do not send it FedEx.

2. If you want to get rich quick, invent a better way of starting the day than having to get up in the morning.

3. No matter what the label says, there is really no such thing as a fat-free Twinkie.

4. Beware of Stairmasters. They only go uphill.

5. If it does not move and it should, use WD-40. If it moves and it should not, use duct tape.

6. Join AAA. Your car's spare tire was never designed for amateurs to remove.

7. Common sense is really . . . uncommon.

Next to the Bible, the greatest sources of wisdom in my life have generally come via subscription. Today, few of our printed materials are fit to read. My grandparents would consider most of today's magazines X-rated—yet many of our young people turn to these same sources to find their identities. How should I act? What should I wear? What are the acceptable sexual standards? The list goes on and on.

Parents, I suggest that you read what your children are reading to see if the contents are biblical. The images and ideas that your child puts into his or her mind make a difference—a big one.

PRINCIPLE: Be aware! Satan often launches a sneak attack on your children through their eyes and thoughts.

PRAYER: *Dear Father, when I was younger, I used to sing a song that said "Oh, be* *careful little eyes what you see." Still, I did not realize how important it was to guard the input to my mind through what I saw, watched, or read. Today, I struggle with these things. Please help me be the guardian of my children's eyes, and shelter them from things that will harm them. Amen.*

DAY FIVE: MAKING A MOUNTAIN OUT OF A MOLE HILL

READING: *Train up a child in the way he should go, and when he is old he will not depart from it* (Proverbs 22:6).

OBSERVATION: I once read a story about a medical student working toxicology at the Poison Control Center. A lady called, very upset because her daughter had eaten ants. The student quickly reassured her that this was not harmful. However, the mother mentioned in passing that she had fed her daughter some ant poison. Immediately, the student reversed his advice and told her to take her daughter to the emergency room right away! Sometimes the cure is worse than the disease.

Years ago, I attended a conference in Florida. When I left Tulsa, I wasn't feeling very good. By the time I landed in Dallas, I was certain that death was imminent. During my layover, I called my doctor, who phoned in a prescription that he told me to take with some over-the-counter medicine. I couldn't swallow the cure fast enough. On the next flight, I spent most of my time on my knees hugging the toilet. If you have ever been in an airplane restroom, you understand how miraculous that really was.

I reached the conference center and locked myself in my room. The more medicine I took, the worse I felt. Finally, I decided to read the back of the over-the-counter medicine bottle. In tiny print, it said, "Do not take with (the name of the medicine my doctor had prescribed)." Within twenty minutes of stopping the other medicine, I was . . . healed. Sometimes the cure *is* the problem.

In my work with families, I have noticed: sometimes the discipline causes more problems than the problem itself. Make sure the consequences you give are . . . logical. As we say in Missouri, "Don't make a mountain out of a molehill." Let me make several suggestions:

1. *Determine which issues are big and which are small.* A child who can't find a sock or spills a glass of water should be treated differently than a child who back-talks or has a spirit of defiance. A gentle correction sounds very different than a

rebuke. Use only as much discipline as needed, because an excess becomes . . . punishment.

2. *Wait to respond.* Tell your child you want to meet with him in an hour. Get away, and spend time praying and seeking counsel. Another perspective often brings wisdom.

3. *Include teaching in your discipline. Training* separates discipline from punishment. Ask your child, "The next time this happens, how should you respond?" Build bridges instead of walls to gain long-term benefits.

Yes, I have changed doctors. I don't want a solution that becomes the problem, or cure that becomes the . . . disease!

PRINCIPLE: Make sure to incorporate *training* when you discipline your child. Otherwise, the solution may become the problem.

PRAYER: *Dear Father, as a parent, I pray that today, You will give me the wisdom of Solomon and the graciousness of Barnabas. Teach me, Lord, to discipline my children correctly. Father, may I be the kind of parent who looks just like . . . You. Amen.*

GRACE DEPOSITS

GOALS, SESSION FIVE:

1. Learners will understand and identify the need to provide children with grace deposits *(statements or actions that communicate an individual's intrinsic worth and value in a way that he finds meaningful)*.

2. Learners will begin to embrace the idea that, as good parents who seek the ancient paths, they will want to provide grace deposits for their children.

3. Learners will understand and commit to forming a grace team *(those people who can consistently make a positive difference in a child's life through words and actions that affirm, support, and build his true identity)* for their child. The team will consist of designated grace depositors *(people chosen to pour grace deposits into a child's life)*.

 **FACILITATORS:** Before this session, please visit **www.ropparenting.com** and download the Session Five ROPPcast. This vidcast contains the *How It Shows* Bible teaching with Walker Moore to use later in the session.

FACILITATORS: Although the study is winding down at this point, the information contained in these final sessions is critical to the overall ROPP process. Encourage attendance, participation, and engagement with the material. Continue to model and openly discuss your own application of the ROPP materials. Be sure to check out the Facilitators' Helps at www.ropparenting.com. Remember that one of your primary tasks is to continue communicating the ROPP message to moms and dads: *You are a good parent. Applying the ROPP principles can help make you an even better one!*

MAKE YOURSELF AT HOME

The fourth and final essential experience of Rite of Passage Parenting is so important that, until now, I've told you more than once, DO NOT TRY THIS AT HOME . . . YET. I'm happy to tell you that the "yet" arrives . . . now! The teaching in this session will prepare you to go back and add a rite of passage, significant tasks, and logical consequences into your family's life in the very best way possible—according to the will and the Word of God. You already know how important I believe these experiences are. I am convinced that the reason I see them repeated in cultures all over the world is because they belong to the ancient path God has placed within us. However, we have also learned that Satan likes to take God's good gifts and make them bad—twisting and turning them so that we willingly accept substitutes that fall far short of His intentions.

What is so essential that experiences as essential as rite of passage, significant tasks, and logical consequences are incomplete without it? What helps remove the sting from the discipline you administer as you raise and train your children according to ROPP? The answer to these questions is the fourth essential experience in ROPP: *grace deposits.*

As I began learning about the cultural shift, I realized more and more that I could observe it right in my own church. As we moved from an agricultural to an industrial society, people moved farther and farther away from extended family members. No longer could mom and dad depend on grandma and grandpa's advice or assistance when they had a need. Now, grandma and grandpa lived far away—and day-to-day parenting problems can't be fixed in a weekend visit or long-distance call. Mom and dad

turned instead to parenting "experts" like Dr. Spock.
Today, experts abound—but so do incapable,
irresponsible, dependent young adults.

*We all learned our parenting skills somewhere. Where do
you think your parents got theirs? What mentor or model
affected the ways they carried out their parenting? Your list
may include a particular baby or child care book, a parenting
expert, a family member, neighbor, friend, pastor, Bible
study, etc.*

What did a lack of contact between generations
have to do with my church? I noticed that the students
in my youth group and the senior adult ministry
operated completely independently of each other.
Because of the cultural shift, neither young people nor
their older counterparts had experience in relating to
one another. To make matters worse, neither group
seemed to know—or care—what it was missing.

I designed an experiment intended to increase
students' understanding of the aging process. One
Sunday afternoon in February, I took some time to
transform the members of my youth group into senior

citizens. I put double layers of gauze over their eyes to obstruct their vision, tied their legs together with short ropes to make them hobble, and even encased their hands with plastic bags to restrict their movement.

Very quickly, the students understood the aches, pains, headaches, and hassles of bodies suffering the effects of age. They also developed a deep compassion for the senior adults whose bodies permanently reflected these changes. The night after we conducted the first experiment in aging, our students visited the senior adults in the church to deliver Valentine flowers. They returned with story after story of laughter and meaningful conversations. The new compassion they felt for their elders had translated into understanding words and actions. Once the senior citizens realized that the young people genuinely cared, they were much more willing to respond with kindness.

The blessings multiplied as the students spent more time with their senior adult friends. In turn, the senior adults became the students' biggest champions and cheerleaders. The experiment in aging worked both forward and backward, and we repeated it every year. It was the beginning of something amazing—something that ROPP calls . . . *grace*.

FACILITATORS: As time allows, ask group members to describe the senior adult who gave them grace. Remind those who did not have such a supporter that it's not their fault—it's the cultural shift.

As a young person, did you have a senior adult who cared about you? If so, write his or her name and relationship (grandparent, neighbor, etc.) here.

What's Missing?

Culture Shock: [Virgil] Gulker is founder and executive director of an unprecedented mentoring program, Kids Hope USA . . . Volunteers from neighborhood churches are paired with an at-risk student and spend an hour a week with him or her at school: reading, doodling, working math problems, shooting hoops, or just listening. The aim is to become the child's friend, a dependable source of encouragement and love.

What has stunned not only teachers and administrators, but Gulker himself, is the payoff from such a meager investment. Teachers consistently report significant improvements in attendance, truancy, and academic achievement.[1]

Culture Shock: I was running with my school in the regional track meet. This was an important meet as we were trying to make it to the state tournament. Personally I wanted to shave off two seconds of my best effort in the 4 X 400 meter relay.

In the event, when I was handed the baton, this guy flew past me, but I was not about to let him go. I pushed my body to the limit, but my heart was bigger than my leg muscle strength. It seemed I fainted. Before I knew what happened, I had fallen facedown on the track.

I was only ten meters from the finish line, but I had lost the baton. I came to quickly and got up, but by the time I had handed off the baton, it was too late. My team ended up finishing in fourth place.

I put my face on the ground and started to cry. I felt miserable—I had given all I had, but I caused my

ROPP TERMS:

GRACE: Statements or actions that help build a child's sense of self-worth and value.

CHECKBOOK THEORY: Parents can systematically and positively affirm their children through grace deposits into an inner spirit account.

GRACE DEPOSITS: Statements or actions that communicate an individual's intrinsic worth in a way that he finds meaningful.

SPIRIT ACCOUNT: A space within each individual from which he draws self-esteem and self-worth.

GRACE DEFICIT: A state in which an individual's spirit account has had more withdrawals than grace deposits so that he sees himself as worthless and insignificant.

team to lose. As I lay there in agony, I felt someone's hand on my back and heard him crying. It was my dad. As I got up, he gave me a great big hug. We embraced and cried together. He kept calling me his cruiser and his prince. I wondered how he could call me his prince after my dismal performance. He said that he had never seen me run so hard and called me a champ.

I went to bed that night worried about what my friends would say at school the next day. Most of them had seen me take the tumble, and surely the ones who hadn't would hear about it. To my surprise the next morning I had a note on my mirror. It was a quote from Teddy Roosevelt that talked about standing strong in the midst of difficulties. My dad had stayed up the night before to find a quote that would encourage me. This meant the world to me![2]
—Fred A. Hartley III

You can probably tell by now that I like analogies. The one I use for the fourth essential experience, *grace deposits,* clearly illustrated by both quotes given here, comes from the banking world. I base this on what I call the *checkbook theory.* Remember the bank and its funny little rule? You'll need to keep that in mind for your parenting too. As you interact with your child, you must make more *grace deposits* than withdrawals, or his *spirit account* will end up in deficit—*grace deficit,* to be exact.

GRACE BANKING

	7777
Your Child's Spirit Account	51%
PAY TO THE ORDER OF Your Child's Name	$ GRACE
1. Eye to Eye 2. Use his name 3. Use deposit language	
	Grace Depositors

Look back at the "Culture Shock" quotes just under the "What's Missing" heading on page 143. In these stories, who gave the grace deposits? Who received them? What impact did the deposits have?

In the days prior to the cultural shift, grandparents were the ones who kept the grace banking system going. Parents, by God's design, are *law* for their kids. They're the ones who teach "no" and "don't," who make the rules and apply the discipline. Grandparents, according to God's ancient path, are givers of *grace*. They get away with slipping Little Johnny an extra dollar or two when Mom and Dad take away his allowance. They always have a hug and a listening ear for Little Susie. Their lives, their words, and their actions model grace for their grandchildren. That's the way God planned it.

Today, however, this picture of grandparents is more the exception than the rule. A growing number of grandparents today have been forced into the "law" role by default because they have to act as parents for their own grandchildren. Families have been caught in the shift, and kids are the innocent victims. In other families, grandparents just don't seem to have the time or interest to act like

LAW: Statements or actions that lessen a child's sense of self-worth and value.

FACILITATORS: If you did not read the "Culture Shock" quotes aloud, take time to do that now. Discuss these in as little or as much detail as time allows, keeping in mind that you are using these examples only to introduce the concept of grace deposits.

grandparents. They've sold the family home, bought an RV, and are traveling the country with a bumper sticker that says, "Out spending my children's inheritance." That attitude (along with the fact that I enjoy watching people's reactions), is one of the reasons I like to say, "Grandparents are the downfall of America."

Do you agree? Are grandparents the downfall of America? Write "yes" or "no" here, then talk with your spouse or your group about ways grandparents have changed since your childhood.

Let's return to the bank for a moment. When Mom and Dad tell Little Johnny to do his homework or take out the trash, they are making a withdrawal from his spirit account. The application of law, no matter how good or right, represents a withdrawal every time.

Please don't misunderstand me: I'm not saying that law is bad. Law keeps things orderly and safe. In fact, God set up an entire code of laws—the ones you probably know as the Ten Commandments—designed to lead us along His ancient paths. However, if you study the Bible further, you will find that God's dealings with His children show a perfect balance of law and grace. He disciplines, but He also blesses. He judges, but He also forgives. He set a high price to pay for our wrong actions, but He also sacrificed His Son to pay for those wrongs by His sacrificial death.

Parents today have a hard time balancing law and grace in their homes. Our lives and schedules are so busy that it's easy to neglect the grace side of interactions with our kids. We can give grace deposits through our words and actions—but sometimes, we make huge withdrawals through the very same means. Without the extra input from grandparents who add grace to a child's life, his spirit account can end up in deficit. That's why I say that grace deposits, like the three other essential experiences, are often missing from kids' lives today. When withdrawals regularly exceed the grace deposits, kids' lives end up . . . bankrupt.

DADSPEAK: *It is easy to look back upon my years of parenting and wish I could go back and do a better job. The problem is that we only get one chance with each child. I pray that by the grace of God, my children will overcome my failures.*

My wife and I are simple people. We lived in the same small, modest home for more than twenty years. Our bedroom faced the street, and the previous owners had planted evergreen bushes in front of the windows to provide privacy.

As the years went by, these bushes grew taller and fuller. After ten years, we decided to cut them down to make the front of our home more inviting. I got out the ax and began chopping away. Few things make a man feel more like a real man than standing in the front yard waving an ax.

As the bushes came tumbling down, I noticed something unusual: papers, lots of them, hidden against the side of the house. Curious, I picked one up. It was Jeremiah's math paper with a low grade penciled at the top. I picked up another one. Again, it was a school paper with a less-than-perfect score. All the papers were from Jeremiah's elementary school years, and they all contained mistakes.

At the time, Jeremiah was a high school student. When I asked him about the papers, he explained that he did not want to show us his failures. Every day, he took out any assignments that he felt were not perfect and hid them behind the bush. For some reason, he believed we would think less of him if he had a bad grade.

Bottom line: he thought he had to earn our approval. I now refer to that bush as the "failure bush." The term does not signify Jeremiah's failure, but my own. That moment of discovery was a great time for me to share with my son that his worth was based on who he was, not what he did. He could never grow to be the man God wanted him to be until he learned to accept and live with failure.

I also have a failure bush. I leave my failures there, and my heavenly Father does not think any less of me. Instead, He forgives and loves me. I find comfort in that failure bush—the one that looks just like . . . a cross.

Among young people today, bankrupt lives are far too common. Bankrupt lives come nowhere close to being capable, responsible, and self-reliant, because bankrupt lives don't care. Kids with bankrupt lives feel like leftovers—unused, unwanted, forgotten, and shoved to the back of the refrigerator shelf.

God's refrigerator, however, contains no leftovers! God tells us that each of us is uniquely designed, with a special plan and purpose that follows His ancient paths (see Psalm 139). Kids who feel like leftovers are missing that fourth essential experience: grace deposits. Satan has twisted the truth, telling them their lives have no purpose or meaning, confusing them about who they are and what they can do. His lies drive their account farther and farther into the red.

There's just one problem, though. Satan was never very good at math, and his figures never quite add up. On the other hand, God's system of grace banking operates in perfect balance. That's because His ways are perfect, and His ancient paths are . . . right.

How It Shows

Culture Shock:

55 . . . percent of grandparents who are "companionate." They enjoy being around their grandchildren and say they love them, but take no real responsibility for them.

29 . . . percent of grandparents who are physically or emotionally "remote" from their grandchildren.

16 . . . percent of American grandparents who are "involved." They spend larger quantities of time with their grandchildren and exercise "a form of parental influence" over them.[3]

10 . . . percent of grandparents responsible for raising at least one grandchild for a period of 6 months.[4]

You see it in the numbers: ever since the agricultural-industrial shift, true grandparents seem to be an endangered species. This lack of intergenerational relationships has left our kids' spirit accounts sadly lacking in grace deposits. When that happens, our bankrupt kids are . . . graceless.

Facilitators:

Facilitators who downloaded it will want to play the Bible teaching segment of the Session Five ROPPcast here. Whether or not you use this option, please go over the Bible teaching in the next few paragraphs and prepare to explain or read alongside your group and/or partner.

One of the most familiar of Jesus' disciples knew exactly what that was like. We can all identify with Peter because he didn't always . . . get it right. He spoke out of turn. He made impulsive decisions. He even turned his back on Jesus—the One he had so boldly said he would never deny.

In Luke 22, we see that before Peter reached that point of denial, he made a *careless commitment.* Yes, he did love Jesus—but he spoke much too rashly (v. 33). Not long after making this careless commitment, Peter demonstrated something else that we all identify with at one time or another: *declining devotion.* Peter's passionate love for Christ seemed to fade farther and farther into the background, and he followed "at a distance" (v. 54) as His eternal plan and earthly enemies propelled Jesus toward the cross. Finally, Peter's downward spiral progressed to the point that he was sharing a meal with the very people who had plotted to kill his Master. Suddenly, we find Peter *eating with the Enemy* (v. 55). When he denies Jesus for the third time, turning away and weeping bitterly, I think we can accurately describe Peter as . . . graceless.

At one time or another, we all feel graceless. Use this space to record such a time in your life (for example, "when I flunked out of college, my family rejected me and I felt as if no one cared").

Thankfully, Peter's story does not end at the point of denial. Jesus later sent a special message to him through the Marys who visited the empty tomb (Luke 29:4–12). I had always wondered why Jesus said, "Go tell the disciples . . . and Peter" (Mark 16:7) that He had risen from the dead. After all, Peter *was* a disciple, wasn't he?

When I understood the checkbook theory, I finally got it. Graceless, friendless Peter, his spirit account in grace deficit, had doubtless stopped considering himself as one of the disciples. I picture him sitting, head in his hands, as the Marys pounded on his door with a message of hope and . . . grace. Later, the Savior sent another huge grace deposit Peter's way when He cooked a restoration meal (a traditional element in Jewish culture) on the shores of the Sea of Tiberias (John 21). To the other disciples, that early-morning fish feast may have looked like breakfast. To Peter, jumping eagerly out of the boat and rushing to meet his Master on the shore, it looked just like . . . a grace deposit.

During the time of gracelessness you described in your answer to the previous question, did God provide people to make grace deposits and help bring your account out of deficit? If so, list the initials of one or two grace depositors here.

ROPP TERMS:

COUNTERFEIT GRACE:
False or misleading
deposits into a spirit
account that cause it to
appear full but add no
genuine value.

IDENTITY: An individual's
accurate self-understanding
of his God-given, unique
attributes.

ROPP: A graceless
teenager whose
spirit account has zeroed
out alienates himself from
family relationships. At
this point, the teen is most
susceptible to the lure of a
gang or cult. Both of these
subgroups offer the
addition of counterfeit
grace by providing the
teen with the accepting,
approving, affirming words
and actions he craves.
Since these kids either do
not get or do not perceive
that they get adequate
grace deposits from their
parents and extended

When kids are graceless, like Peter before his time of restoration and hope, they end up with empty spirit accounts. Even kids whose parents have tried to raise them right—especially those living in the shadow of the cultural shift—are vulnerable to Satan's assaults. He attacks their thoughts through various sensory inputs, and his whispers serve as huge grace withdrawals (*"Why can't you ever. . .?" "How come you never . . .?"*) He works overtime to push their spirit accounts over into the red, leaving them spiritually, morally, and emotionally . . . bankrupt.

When Peter's account went into grace deficit, he turned very quickly to eating with the Enemy—an artificial means of filling his account. Deep down, Peter knew this relationship was not truly fulfilling; and deep down, our kids know their wrong relationships and activities are empty too. Like the rest of Satan's lies, artificial ways to fill a spirit account appear meaningful but hold no true value. That's why *Rite of Passage Parenting* calls them . . . *counterfeit grace.*

Today, counterfeit grace takes various forms. One of the most obvious of these is what psychologists call "peer dependence," in which a young person, confused about who he is, looks to his peers to determine his *identity*. Research shows that these confused young people experience—and often act out—a strong pressure to conform to the group.

Peer dependence: we've all experienced it. If it hasn't shown up in the lives of your kids yet—just wait. On the following scales, with 1 being low (not at all dependent on peers to determine attitudes, actions, beliefs, and values) and 10 being high (extremely dependent on peers to determine attitudes, actions, beliefs, and values), rate your level of peer dependence as a fifteen-year-old, then your oldest child's level of peer dependence at the same age (if he has reached it) or today. If you are part of a group, share answers as time allows.

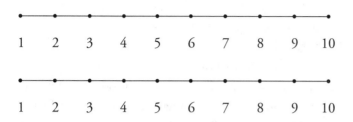

Technology! Parents today know it as a blessing and a curse. The same technology that allows you to check in at home while running errands after work or shuttling kids from one activity to another also has the potential to keep your kids tuned-in, turned-on . . . and turned-off, it seems, to any genuine attempts at communication. Multitasking teens fill their spirit accounts with so much counterfeit grace from cell phones, iPods, computers, and other technological tools that they often have trouble connecting with parents or other adults in person. Even worse, all this multitasking takes up vast amounts of time and energy. It falsely fills so much space in a spirit account that often, young people mistrust the validity of genuine grace deposits. If we give them, our kids may fail to receive them. A grace deposit thus becomes a withdrawal, and kids' spirit accounts sink deeper into . . . grace deficit.

Technology also enables even more dangerous grace deficits through Facebook, MySpace, and other social Internet sites geared to young people. Regular news stories confirm the frightening realities of sexual predators and pornographic images that users of these sites can innocently—or not-so-innocently—

family, they seek them elsewhere. (*Rite of Passage Parenting*) encounter. Young people post pictures, personal information, and private thoughts online; desperately seeking validation from others' responses. Although this may seem harmless at first, anyone who seeks identity primarily through this "MySpace Grace" exposes himself to the potential for devastating withdrawals.

That kind of withdrawal can leave a spirit . . . bankrupt. When an individual loses his identity, he loses a genuine understanding of who he is and where he is going. He also opens himself up—just as the graceless Peter did when he lost his identity as a disciple—for some of the Enemy's most damaging attacks.

Think about a graceless young person you know. (Those who have a child who falls or has fallen into this category may share their personal experience or speak about someone else if they wish.) Without naming the individual, write a few words to explain any evidence for "how it shows" in his life.

When Peter lived as a graceless loser instead of a faithful disciple, he showed that he had lost his identity: he didn't know who he was, so he didn't know what to do. When our kids do the same today, they trade the truth of the ancient paths for a modern lie. We can see ample evidence for this in the area of relationship. Dad, if you don't provide grace deposits for your daughter, she'll find someone who will: a hormonally imbalanced, knuckle-dragging ape who won't look or act anything like the man you hope and pray she'll find one day. Mom, you have a responsibility to provide plenty of grace deposits for your son's account too. The Enemy lurks around the corner and on the other side of the modem, waiting to lure his heart and fill his mind with inappropriate images and unfulfilling relationships.

An individual who experiences a loss of identity through grace withdrawals has already begun to step away from his *authority*. When Peter gradually backed away from Jesus (his authority), he began to reject and rebel against his Master's insight, influence, and input into his life. Rebellion is a dangerous—and graceless—way to live.

ROPP TERMS:

AUTHORITY: A designated person or persons to whom an individual voluntarily submits his will.

BUILDING PROJECT

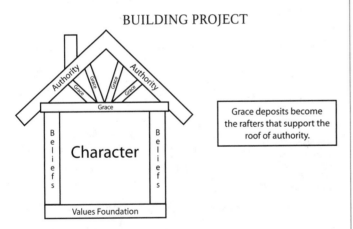

Grace deposits become the rafters that support the roof of authority.

To turn back to our building analogy: authority is the roof that provides protection and direction. A graceless child who tries to slip away from his authority is like a building trying to slip out from under that all-important roof. Sooner or later, something is bound to collapse! That's why, when I

Facilitators: We're getting up close and personal again as we move toward the end of the session. Continue to model open, honest communication, and keep reminding the parents that, regardless of how well they perceive their own handling of the *grace* element of parenting, they are good parents who are seeking to become even better ones.

draw this picture once more, I show grace deposits as the rafters. They support the authority and make it harder for the building beneath them to slip and slide. A child whose life is not supported by enough grace rafters can ease out from under the roof of authority, exposed and vulnerable to every storm.

How does the lack of grace deposits show? An empty spirit account—a bankrupt life—a collapsed building. Be sure to keep reading so you can find ways to incorporate grace banking into your family by adding grace deposits and subtracting . . . heartache.

Ask God to help you think back on your life as you were growing up. Did you receive enough grace deposits to keep your spirit account from going into deficit? On the following scale, -10 (grace deficit) to + 10 (filled to overflowing), mark where you think your spirit account balance rested at age 5, 10, and 15.

```
•——•——•——•——•——•——•——•——•——•——•——•——•——•——•——•——•——•——•——•——•
-10                      0                    +10
GRACE DEFICIT               FILLED TO OVERFLOWING
```

 ## #4: Establish Their True Identity Through Grace Deposits

Grandparents have gone missing from our culture, and with them have gone vast amounts of grace deposits. On every side, in this and every way, the Enemy tries to take away our kids' sense of identity, leaving their spirit accounts in deficit and their character building collapsed.

What can we do? I think we need to start where Jesus always started when He had a need: on His knees, in the place of prayer. That's where Cathy and I found ourselves during a challenging time in our lives. We had recently moved to Tulsa, where I had taken on a new church staff position. This job—like almost any ministry—required time and energy that often came at the expense of our family. Since we were new in town, we hadn't yet had much time to build friendships. On top of that, we lost two grace-giving grandparents within the space of a year—first my mother, then Cathy's dad. Cathy and I, in the midst of our pain, began to pray about our boys and how we could keep them from growing up . . . graceless.

Very often, God's answer to prayer comes in the form of a person. In this case, His answer was a very special person: a godly widow at our church named Lucile Hodges. Lucile, a retired schoolteacher, helped me out in an emergency one day by taking care of Caleb when Cathy was out of town. The two of them bonded immediately (I think it had something to do with candy bars) with a love that soon extended to the rest of our family. We had lost two grandparents, but we gained a very special adopted mom and grandma in the form of Lucile. Through the years, she has become one of the strongest encouragers, greatest supporters, and most generous grace depositors we have ever known. God's answer to our prayer was full of . . . grace.

Do you have a Lucile? Here, please share a few words about a grandparent or other grace depositor who has played an important role in your life and/or your children's lives.

ROPP: I did not know Lucile, and I had not learned these principles when my sons were born. Today, I encourage you to surround your child—from the day of birth onward—with people who can consistently make a positive difference in his life: a grace team. As soon as you know that God is preparing to bless you with a child, begin praying with your mate about whom He intends to place on this child's grace team. This group of people will pour God's grace into your child's life, especially during those many times when mom and dad must be . . . law. *(Rite of Passage Parenting)*

God's answer to your prayer for grace for your children can come in the form of *designated grace depositors*. Some of these, like a teacher or coach, will have temporary input into your child's life. Others, like Lucile, will form part of a specially chosen *grace team* who will support your child from birth onward, helping add grace deposits into his life that will keep his spirit account full and his life from bankruptcy. See Fix-It #5-1 on page 167 for more specific suggestions on forming a grace team.

MomSpeak: *Walker's statement that "Grandparents are the downfall of America" confused me at first. My own parents have done a great job of being long-distance grandparents to our five. They stay in touch with cards, notes, and extra gifts that provide grace deposits in special "only from Grandma and Grandpa" ways. Tom's parents and grandmother did much the same before they passed away. Sadly, I understand now that grandparents like this are more the exception than the rule today. I see the evidence all around me.*

However, I also realized that another reason I held such a high view of grandparents was that, as a pastor's family, God has blessed our children with grace depositors in every church we've served. These dear people have taken special interest in our kids. Their deposits have taken varied forms, from outings, to the provision of significant tasks and affirmation for jobs well-done, to extra attention and gifts at just the right time.

Like the Moores, our family has benefited from a chosen grace team. Our kids not only have an adopted grandma— they have two loving adopted grandparents. Grandma Lou and Grandpa Benny have visited us in each one of our homes, enjoyed countless games and stories with our kids, and joined us at many family milestone events.

Most importantly, they have modeled faith, commitment, and unconditional love to the Piepers long before any of our children were born. No wonder we love them so much! The ties between us come not through genetics, but by grace.

What about you? Just because you form a grace team for your child does not take away your responsibility for making grace deposits into his life. In fact, as a Rite of Passage Parent, you will need to understand grace deposits very well. You'll want to explain their use to your child's grace team—and, of course, you'll want to continue giving them to your spouse, your children, and anyone else whose life intersects yours. As you continue your own process of maturing, you want to grow up to look more and more like Jesus. Read the New Testament, and you'll see immediately that, although He was a perfect fulfillment of the law, His life was also marked by . . . grace.

*Although Jesus exemplified both, our personalities and spiritual gifts tend to move us toward either the "law" or the "grace" side of parenting. Where are you? Use the scale below to indicate where you think you fall on the law (right) or grace (left) side. Does your spouse agree? Mark this answer with an **S** if so.*

-10   0   + 10

LAW   GRACE

WHAT ARE THE ODDS? I was attending a statewide Christian conference when God began calling me to overseas ministry. This seemed overwhelming to a backwoods country girl with little stability in her life. I was only fifteen, but I had

ROPP TERMS:

DESIGNATED GRACE DEPOSITORS: Someone chosen to pour grace deposits into a child's life.

GRACE TEAM: Those people who can consistently make a positive difference in a child's life through words and actions that affirm, support, and build his true identity.

survived my parents' divorce; my mom's relationship with another man, who was an alcoholic; and changing schools about eight times. My demeanor was extremely shy, and fear controlled most of my actions.

God continued to nudge me when Walker Moore, the conference speaker, talked about the needs and opportunities of international missions. I was afraid to acknowledge this call even to myself—much less to an auditorium of 3,000 students—but my mother saw the truth and began (almost literally) moving me toward it. A short time later, we happened to be in the same room as Walker. Mom unexpectedly pushed me into him, telling him that God had called me to go!

Especially because my family was in such turmoil, I am thankful that people like Walker began to give me grace deposits. His words about what God could accomplish through my life allowed me to look beyond my immediate situation. My youth leader made many more grace deposits to my spirit account. She repeatedly told me that she believed God had given me a special calling and confirmed the burden that God had placed on my heart for international ministry. She continued encouraging me by saying she believed I would become a person who made a difference in the world. My pastor gave me additional grace deposits, affirming God's call on my life and promising His support to help move me toward that call.

Perhaps these grace deposits don't seem very dramatic, but they were extremely reassuring to a fearful and insecure young woman. As I followed the wise counsel of these grace depositors and traveled overseas, I realized my true worth. I saw, probably for the first time, that God could use even someone like me in amazing, life-changing ways.

Today, my husband and I lead an organization,

Breaking Borders, that takes people overseas to help those in need. I try to give grace deposits to those I serve and work alongside. When I think back, I realize that these simple words and actions from people who believed in me have shaped the person I am today. —Peggy Nunley[5]

You understand the idea of grace deposits. You've seen examples of the way they work—and what happens when kids don't have enough of them in their lives. But how exactly do you give a grace deposit? Once you know the answer to this question, you'll be ready to go back and *try this at home.*

1. LOOK AT THEM EYE TO EYE. Looking another person in the eye indicates that he or she has your full attention. Not long ago, a friend's little daughter tried to speak with him while he watched a televised sporting event. After repeated attempts to break the lure of the game, she grasped his chin and turned his face toward hers, saying, "Daddy! Listen with your eyes!" Giving visual contact—listening with your eyes—tells your kids they matter. That's a great way to begin depositing . . . grace.

2. USE THEIR NAMES. When you attempt to add grace deposits to your children's spirit accounts, make sure you use their names. Names matter to God. He gave names as a part of His act of creation, giving Adam the significant task of naming the animals. The act of naming signifies lordship or authority over someone or something else.

Individual names hold special meaning. Jesus used names when He called His disciples. Sometimes, He even renamed them to recast their character and move them into their true identity. God has been in the "renaming" business for a long time, in fact. Ever heard of Jacob/Israel, Simon/Peter, Saul/Paul? Names carry worth and value. Names are important. Names signify . . . grace deposits.

Do you remember the principle of expectation? If your child believes that no one expects very much from her, she will tend to live up to that expectation. On the other hand, if she knows that people expect great things, she will be much more likely to become . . . great.

If your child's name carries a negative connotation, it may be time to give her a new one. I practice that with my Awe Star students all the time. Sometimes, their names have been used to administer so much law that just hearing their name spoken is a huge grace withdrawal. I've seen some amazing results from renaming students like this with names that reveal their worth and value. A meaningful name becomes a grace deposit every time you use it. Make sure you do.

Take time to think for a few moments about your own name. If you know its meaning, write it here. If you know why your parents gave you the name they did, write the reason here as well.

3. USE DEPOSIT LANGUAGE. The world of banking has its own special language, and so does the world of grace banking. When you give your child a grace deposit, make sure to use *deposit language*. Names hold negative connotations, but so do other words. Don't make the mistake of withdrawing grace when you mean to deposit it. Using appropriate words—deposit language—will complete the deposit every time.

Remembering to use one special word—*because*—will make a great start. "I appreciate you *because* you helped your brother get ready for school without anybody asking you." "I really admire you *because* you came home talking about the needs of other kids." "I appreciate you today *because* you helped get the dinner table ready tonight. That was a big help to your mom."

Generic compliments like "You're so wonderful" or "You're really special," no matter how well-intended, always end up as withdrawals. When kids (and adults) hear a generic compliment, their minds often begin to work overtime to take away its value: ("I'm not pretty! My nose is too big!" or "No way am I smart. I just flunked a math test!"). Using the word "because" makes the compliment specific and helps keep Satan from whispering lies to your kids about who they are or what they do.

 ROPP TERMS:

DEPOSIT LANGUAGE: Words that add grace deposits to a spirit account.

GRACE BANKING

		7777
Your Child's Spirit Account	51%	
PAY TO THE ORDER OF Your Child's Name	$ GRACE	
1. Eye to Eye 2. Use his name 3. Use deposit language		
	Grace Depositors	

FACILITATORS: Provide a bowl of M & Ms or similar treat. Pass it around and encourage everyone to take a specific amount of candy to reflect the number of children in his family—either the one he grew up in, or the number of children he has now. No one is to eat his candy until the exercise is complete. After everyone has taken an appropriate number of candies, explain that the number of treats they have will be the number of grace deposits they will now give to the person on their left.

Lead the group to move clockwise around the room to share these deposits. Take your turn first, being careful to model proper deposit mode: look the recipients in the eye, use their names, use deposit language. "Just do it." For example, turn to Eddie and say, "I admire you, Eddie, because you always come prepared for our lesson." "I appreciate you, Eddie,

4. JUST DO IT. My deposit instructions have placed a strong emphasis on what you *say*. All good parents know, however, that parenting goes far beyond what you say. You show who you are as a parent by what you *do*.

My son, Jeremiah, loves few things better than professional basketball. During his growing-up years, my wife made a special effort to *do* something for him that would deposit plenty of grace into his account. She asked Jeremiah for a list of his favorite basketball players and their nicknames. Now, Cathy cares much more about our boys than she does about basketball, but she spent hours memorizing that list. Jeremiah was so proud of her accomplishments! He loved to invite his friends over and have his mom surprise them with her amazing knowledge of Karl "The Mailman" Malone or Charles "The Chuck Wagon" Barkley. Cathy's loving act communicated worth and value to Jeremiah. What she *did* had become a grace deposit.

Rite of Passage Parents will learn to *do*, as well as to say, the things that their kids find meaningful. One child may love watching old movies with mom or dad. Another may prefer that you take her along when you run errands. Still another finds it meaningful when you value what he values—the way Cathy did when she memorized Jeremiah's basketball list. Remember? Grace deposits begin—and end—in the place of prayer. Ask God to show you ways to give grace deposits that will matter most to your kids . . . and fill their spirit accounts to overflowing.

You've been studying the ROPP principles in this workbook for five weeks now. If you're studying as part of a group, God has used this time to draw you closer to the other good parents around you. Take a few moments to write down

some genuine grace deposits—qualities or characteristics you admire, stated in deposit language—about the person to your left. Your facilitator will instruct you about how and when to share these.

because you spend so much time playing board games with your children."

 51 PERCENT: This week, concentrate on the following *ROPP* handles:

1. Review and reread any sections in the ROPP Workbook that continue to challenge you. List these areas here.

2. Your next step, like giving grace deposits, begins with prayer. Take time to pray and then begin to list the individuals you (and your spouse, if possible) would choose to enlist to serve on a grace team of grace depositors for your child or children. Be ready to explain why you would choose these individuals, especially if you are studying this workbook as part of a group.

FACILITATORS: If time allows, ask members to share about the other side of the bank balance: how it felt to receive these grace deposits. Encourage them to keep "trying this at home" now that they've learned to give grace deposits the right way.

3. *Begin now to "TRY THIS AT HOME" by giving grace deposits to your spouse and your children this week. Fix-It #2, page 168, gives you a set of blank grace deposit checks designed to help as you complete this task. (Additional grace deposit checks are available as a free download at www.ropparenting.com.) Every day, as you finish a ROPP devotion, fill in a check. Every day, fill it in with the name of someone in your family to whom you will give a grace deposit. (Use a different name every day until you have given grace deposits to all family members; then begin again. If you have a large family, you may need to use more than one "grace check" every day!) Make sure to use deposit language and to follow the other principles taught in the final section of this session.*

4. *Over a five-day period before beginning the next session, read and study the five-day ROPP Devotion Guide that follows the Fix-Its for this chapter. Next, complete the following: This ROPP Workbook reminds you regularly that you are a good parent. Which of this week's devotional readings helped you the most in your journey toward becoming an even better one? Write its title here and a few words about why or how it helped.*

FIX-IT #5-1:
FORMING A GRACE TEAM FOR YOUR CHILD

ROPP SUMMARY: The cultural shift has affected our families in many ways. No longer do ladies get together to hold quilting bees or men gather to help one another bring in the crops or raise a barn. In the past, extended family members provided grace for children. In addition, entire communities of people with similar values and beliefs gathered for social interaction and the communication of intergenerational grace.

Today, we encourage you to surround your family's life with a personally selected, intergenerational community known as the *grace team:* those people who can consistently make a positive difference in a child's life through words and actions that affirm, support, and build his true identity. How do you find this team? What qualities should you look for as you form it?

ROPP SOLUTION: The grace team begins in the place of prayer. Pray (with your spouse, if possible) for your child and for these special people. Ask God to show you who can become godly influencers in your child's life and to bring people toward you who have the following qualities:

Gracious: humble, caring, kind, and generous in word and deed.

Reverent: holding to and practicing the principles of Scripture. Committed to following God's will and Word.

Admired: a respected influencer of others; demonstrating honor and integrity.

Compassionate: other-centered rather than self-centered; concerned for the needs and welfare of those around them.

Established: having the personal experience and history that demonstrates a sound life.

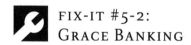

FIX-IT #5-2:
GRACE BANKING

The following blank checks can be used as God reminds you of grace deposits to give your children. Learn to celebrate your children's successes—from the small ones, like helping a younger sibling fix her hair, to the big ones, like graduating from high school. You may want to copy this sheet and use a page or more of checks for each child—especially until grace deposits become more automatic for you, or during a time when you sense that your child has become graceless. Add to his spirit account and watch the balance grow. It may take a while, but one day, the balance will . . . overflow.

ROPP Grace Deposit Slip

Your Child's Spirit Account

August 1
Date

PAY TO THE ORDER OF   David P $

Mom

I appreciate you because you showed kindness to your sister by helping her put her socks on.

Grace Depositors

ROPP Grace Deposit Slip

Your Child's Spirit Account

Date

PAY TO THE ORDER OF $

Grace Depositors

ROPP Grace Deposit Slip

Your Child's Spirit Account

Date

PAY TO THE ORDER OF $

Grace Depositors

ROPP Grace Deposit Slip

Your Child's Spirit Account

Date

PAY TO THE ORDER OF $

Grace Depositors

ROPP Grace Deposit Slip

Your Child's Spirit Account

Date

PAY TO THE ORDER OF $

Grace Depositors

ROPP Grace Deposit Slip

Your Child's Spirit Account

Date

PAY TO THE ORDER OF $

Grace Depositors

RITE OF PASSAGE PARENTING
DEVOTION GUIDE

DAY ONE: THE WORLD'S BEST HAIRSPRAY

READING: *And he brought him to Jesus. Now when Jesus looked at him, He said, "You are Simon the son of Jonah. You shall be called Cephas" (which is translated,* A Stone) (John 1:42).

OBSERVATION: What do you do in a foreign country when you run out of hairspray? In Hungary, no problem! Walk two blocks, catch the tram, and two stops later, you reach a store. I don't really need hairspray except for one misplaced cowlick. If I fail to control it, I walk around looking like Alfalfa from "The Little Rascals."

My normal brand of hairspray is cheap (the key word) and does the trick. One summer, I found myself walking up and down the aisles of that small Hungarian store, trying to find something that resembled . . . hairspray. I found everything from racks of fresh-baked bread to vegetables and milk, but no hairspray.

After more searching, I found a section of personal care products. I could make out some of the words like "szampo" (shampoo) or "kreme" (shaving cream), but saw nothing that looked like "hairspray." I did not recognize any brand names, either, but finally found an aerosol can of stuff I thought might work.

The next morning, I tried my new hairspray and was absolutely amazed. It was far superior to anything back home. That cowlick never even *thought* about standing up. This stuff was definitely in charge!

I began to compliment the locals. "We have nothing like this hairspray in all of America," I proclaimed. They smiled politely, but kept asking me what kind I was using. Since I butchered the Hungarian pronunciation, they did not recognize the product.

One morning, I took the "world's best hairspray" along to show them what I meant. Their reactions ranged from horror to hysteria. "Brother Walker, that is not hairspray! It is . . . underarm deodorant." What a great product—a combination hairspray/deodorant!

The next day, I tried its intended use. You know what it did to my hair, so you can imagine what it did to my underarms. How can the world's best hairspray be the world's worst deodorant? That's life: you have to take the good with the bad.

That's true with our children too. We all have dreams of raising the perfect child, and soon discover a little deodorant mixed with the hairspray.

Did I throw it away? Of course not. The world's best hairspray also kept my head from sweating. Do not get caught up with labels, or you might miss something great on the inside.

PRINCIPLE: Your child's self-perception is based upon the label you give him or her.

PRAYER: *Dear Father, I thank You for the label You have put on my life. You call me a child of the King, a high priest, redeemed, a person of worth, and of value. Today, I confess that I have sometimes put labels on my children out of frustration. May I see them through Your eyes and give them labels that will reflect who they are in You. Amen.*

DAY TWO: LANGUAGE LESSONS FROM LASSIE

READING: *For I have not spoken on My own authority; but the Father who sent Me gave Me a command, what I should say and what I should speak* (John 12:49).

OBSERVATION: I wish I were a great communicator. Not like Billy Graham, even though there is no one who presents the simple plan of salvation like he does. Not even like Zig Ziglar, who can sell gloves to a man with no hands. Not even like the guy who, at three o'clock in the morning, is hawking those space-age mops that can soak up the entire Atlantic Ocean—for the low, low price of only $19.95, limited time offer.

What I want is to be a great communicator like Lassie. Every week, this collie heroine would come running to the screen door and begin to bark. Ruth, (for the TV-illiterate, Timmy was the little boy who was Lassie's master, and Ruth was his mother) would come to the door and say, "Lassie, what's wrong?"

At that point, Lassie would bark three times. Ruth, being fluent in dogspeak, would say, "What, Timmy fell into the well again? He has a fracture of his left tibia? Call 911?" Lassie would bark "Yes," and the next thing you knew, there was Lassie, playing the part of tour guide; leading the doctor, ambulance, parents, and the entire U.S. Army to rescue her boy. Without Lassie, the show would have had only one episode. In the end, Timmy would always give Lassie a huge hug, thanking her for saving his life . . . and the life of the show.

Why is it that when I come home barking, no one, not even my dog, understands what I say? I come from a long line of "barkers." Where is Lassie when you need her, anyway?

Parents were not created to bark, but instead to *communicate.* There are only two verses in the Bible that mention barking. Both refer to a dog. Sometimes *how* you communicate is much more important than *what* you communicate. "A soft answer turns away wrath, but a harsh word stirs up anger" (Proverbs 15:1).

One time, when my youngest son had done something really terrible, I found myself waiting for him to get home so I could "lay into him." The Lord convicted me about my approach. Instead, I confronted him in a soft, loving voice; put my arm around his shoulder; and prayed with him. It touched him so deeply that he thanked me.

Lassie . . . maybe it's time to quit barking after all.

PRINCIPLE: Jesus' Father told Him not only what to say, but how to say it. He will do the same for you.

PRAYER: *Dear Father, it is so easy just to . . . bark. Barking makes me feel better—but it does very little for my children. Help me to communicate in ways that will draw them closer to You and to me. Amen.*

DAY THREE: OIL OF OLÉ

READING: *Ointment and perfume delight the heart, And the sweetness of a man's friend gives delight by hearty counsel* (Proverbs 27:9).

OBSERVATION: It happened in either fifth or sixth grade. For Parents' Night, our class was asked to perform a Mexican dance. The teacher assigned parts according to each child's grace and agility—and I had earned the best one of all! For weeks, I excitedly told my parents all about our rehearsals. I wanted to make sure they would both attend my world premiere.

The moment came. My fellow dancers and I waited behind the closed curtains, which drew slowly apart to reveal an audience of proud parents. I stood on the back row: hand expertly placed on one hip, grin spread from ear to ear, head held high. As the music began, the children in front of me moved forward. Boys and girls intertwined, gracefully swirling and bowing. I held my position, watching. My parents' eyes remained glued to their son, awaiting his special part.

Finally, the music wound down. The other children returned. This was my cue. I walked between them, got down on one knee, threw my arms wide, and yelled . . . "Olé!"

The curtains closed as I held my dramatic position. I hurriedly left the stage, eager to see my parents' pride. As I ran up to them, I sensed that they had been laughing hysterically. Dad kept throwing up his hands and yelling, "Olé, olé!" All the way home, they kept breaking into laughter, repeating, "Olé!"

I never again attempted a school dance.

As an adult, I can see why Mom and Dad thought this was funny. They had waited eagerly for my part, only to have it consist of a single "Olé!" To me, however, dancing wasn't nearly as important as appearing on stage and having the only speaking role . . . especially one that involved a foreign language. What was a Mexican dance without a final "Olé"?

My parents saw it differently . . . they thought I wasn't good enough to dance. My stunning performance was relegated to the joke of the year.

Even to this day, when I think about it, it still hurts a little. Mom and Dad didn't mean to cause me pain. That's my point. A child works hard to draw a picture, only to have a parent say, "What *is* it?" Next time, he doesn't even want to take the crayons out of the box, because he doesn't want to experience . . . more pain.

Would you do me a favor? The next time your child comes home and tells you that he got the best part in the school musical, just agree. Many dreams have been dashed by a careless laugh. Olé?

PRINCIPLE: Words are like tools—they can build up or tear down. Would you prefer to improve a beautiful building, adding to its value and function . . . or destroy it? Use words with your children that are designed to reinforce God's purposes in their lives.

PRAYER: *Lord, help me to be a wise builder. Teach me how to use the right words with my children . . . at the right time and in the right way. Protect them from my thoughtless words and actions. Help me to show them Your love in everything I say and do. Amen.*

DAY FOUR: WORDS MATTER

READING: *Let us think about each other and help each other to show love and do good deeds* (Hebrews 10:24 NCV).

OBSERVATION: Is there really such thing as a *twelve-ounce pound cake*? How about a *paid volunteer*? The way we use the English language has become *explicitly* *ambiguous.* Have you ever referred to something as *pretty ugly*? Or have you given someone a *definite maybe*? Could you call your kitchen *randomly organized*? Consider these word combinations: *tight slacks, exact estimate, peace force, alone together, same difference, child proof, new classic,* or my all-time favorite—*synthetic natural gas.*

One day, as the census taker was making rounds, a five-year-old girl answered the door. She told the visitor that her daddy was a doctor, but that he wasn't home. She added that he was at the hospital performing an appendectomy. "My, that sure is a big word for such a little girl," the census taker said. "Do you know what it means?" "Sure," the little girl answered. "Fifteen hundred bucks, and that doesn't even include the anesthesiologist." Somewhere along the way, this little girl assigned a value to the word *appendectomy.*

Like this little girl, many children assign value to words based upon the context in which they hear them spoken at home. Words are important and should not be tossed around carelessly. It only takes a few seconds for a word to alter a child's perception of the world or of himself. Words spoken in grace and love can cause a child to grow up completely self-assured. On the other hand, a child's life can be completely dismantled by . . . words. One who is constantly surrounded by negative language like, "Why can't you ever do anything right?" or, "Why do I always have to tell you this?" or, "When will you ever learn?" . . . grows up believing the worst about himself.

I can tell you that without an intervention from above, children will live with negative words the rest of their lives. These words and their destructive power rob kids of self-worth, dignity, and potential. Even worse, this type of speech becomes a pattern passed down from generation to generation. Many parents who use adverse language do so because they grew up under its shadow. Without a conscious effort to break the mold, it will continue for generations. The words that you speak today will affect your children, grandchildren, and great-grandchildren.

Ask God to teach you to use language that builds a child's security and self-image. Begin to say "I admire you because . . . ," "I appreciate you because . . . ," and "I love you because."

I hope you do not *clearly misunderstand* what I'm trying to say!

PRINCIPLE: Children receive words as either constructive or destructive. Be wise in the ones you choose.

PRAYER: *Dear Father, please let me hear what I say through the ears of my children. Sometimes I do not realize that the words I am using diminish their identity. Give me words that will build, encourage, and edify them; and that will honor You. Amen.*

DAY FIVE: GOING THROUGH THE GARBAGE

READING: *"Father, I desire that they also whom You gave Me may be with Me where I am, that they may behold My glory which You have given Me; for You loved Me before the foundation of the world"* (John 17:24).

OBSERVATION: Many years ago, I served in a rapidly growing church. In order to acquire more space, the congregation bought five houses. They planned to use four of them for Sunday school classes and tear the fifth one down for parking. This last house had a one-car garage that the previous owners had used only as a garbage dump . . . for the past twenty years! Over time, the trash had compressed it into a solid block about chest-high.

Our church had asked the Fire Marshal if we could burn the garage and garbage, but the answer was "no." I volunteered to haul away the trash as long as I could keep anything I found. On the day they began tearing down the house, I started going through the garbage. As I peeled away the repulsive layers, I discovered a mother lode of antiques, all in pristine condition. I found over one hundred antique Coke bottles, an antique pendulum wall clock that hangs in my living room even today, old glass milk bottles, medical tins, and magazines from the 1950s—all in mint condition.

By the end of the day, I was overwhelmed by all the treasures I had found. That day, God taught me an important principle: underneath the garbage, you will find something of value.

Sharon was beautiful, but she was an alcoholic. She had spent years running from God. While counseling her, I showed her my diamond ring. I told her it was worth $700. Then I picked up some dirt and rubbed it onto the ring. I asked her how much it was worth now, and she replied, "It's worth $700." Then I spit on the ring, mixing the dirt with saliva. I asked her, "How much is it worth now?" She replied again, "It's worth $700." The ring needed cleaning, but the amount of garbage covering it never changed its real value.

I told Sharon that she was the diamond. No matter how much garbage she had in her life, she was still a person of value to God. When you look at your children, do you see the garbage or do you, like God, see . . . the diamond in the rough?

Principle: If you don't see anything of value in your children, they will perceive themselves as garbage.

Prayer: *Dear Father, You love me as much as You love Your own Son. You look past my faults, and because of Your grace, count me worthy of a relationship with You. Today, help me to focus more on my child's worthiness than his or her imperfections. Help me to love my child as You have loved me. Amen.*

~

RITE OF PASSAGE PARENTING
CELEBRATION

GOALS, SESSION SIX:

1. As good parents who seek the ancient paths, learners will embrace the four essential experiences of ROPP as an enduring value in their lives.
2. Learners will celebrate God's work through ROPP and surrender to allowing Him to continue making Himself at home in their hearts, lives, and families; submitting to His authority and to the human ones that He puts in place.
3. Learners will understand and covenant together to support, encourage, and hold one another accountable for their continuing growth as Rite of Passage Parents.

 MAKE YOURSELF AT HOME "STAND BY THE WAYS, AND SEE, AND ASK"

As the session begins (and if you're part of a group, during the time when members are entering the study room), take a few minutes to share which Session Five ROPP

FACILITATORS: Before this session, please visit www.ropparenting.com and download the Session Six ROPPcast. This vidcast contains the *How It Shows* Bible teaching with Walker Moore to use later in the session. Also, I recommend that you make this session a real celebration. For many people (even Bible heroes), celebrations mean . . . food. Ask everyone to bring a favorite dessert or other contribution to a fellowship meal. I admire you because I know you will do whatever it takes to turn this session into a real celebration!

FACILITATORS: The final session of this ROPP Workbook marks an end and a beginning: the end of the regularly scheduled group meetings, and the beginning of a new covenant. Today, these Rite of Passage Parents will surrender to a continuing relationship as designated grace depositors and accountability partners for one another. This session also celebrates the ancient paths set forth in the workbook material and in ROPP, the work God has done in these good parents, and the wonderful plans He has for each of them and for their families. Through the weeks of study together, they have acquired some tools that will help them in raising not just kids, but capable, responsible, self-reliant *adults*.

By the way, you're more than just a good parent—you're a great facilitator! You've led your group into some exciting new areas of thinking and responding

Devotion helped you most in your journey as a good parent. (See pages 169–175 if you need a reminder).

This was the first week in which you began to "try this at home" by adding grace deposits to your spouse's and children's spirit accounts. Now, it's time for an account statement. Write a note here giving the name of one person who received a Grace Banking check from you along with a few words about how they responded to the deposit.

As we begin our study this week, I want to remind you that you are a good parent! You want to "stand by the ways, and see, and ask." That's what you've been doing through the weeks of this study. As my son, Caleb, told me a while back, *"Dad, bad parents don't buy books."* You're taking time to "see and ask" for good and godly answers to help with your parenting. That makes you . . . not just a good parent, but a great one!

Take time now for a Grace Blast. Focus on members one at a time. Have each individual stand in the center of the group and, as quickly as you can, go around the circle to take turns pouring grace deposits into him or her: "Brent, I admire you because you make time to take your daughters on dates." "David, I appreciate you because you keep pouring grace into your daughter even when she rejects you," etc. Have a different member take the center spot at your Facilitator's direction. Spouses studying this book together should make sure to give one another a Grace Blast too. Studying alone? Watch for the Grace Blasts God will bring you through other people now and in days to come!

WHAT'S MISSING?
"THE ANCIENT PATHS, WHERE THE GOOD WAY IS, AND WALK IN IT"

Maybe you're a young parent of very young children. Your kids are sweet and innocent—but you can see the potential for problems ahead, because you know what you faced while you were growing up. Maybe your kids are older. You've had some great days—but some difficult ones too. You are a good parent, but you still have struggles. You've done many things right—but your kids still do wrong. Maybe you're even, like so many people today, a grandparent raising grandchildren in your home. Nearly every day, you face the battles you fought with your kids all over again, complicated by the overwhelmingly negative influences of multiple media inputs and the widespread decline in moral standards.

Regardless of what your family looks or acts like, you should understand by now that it's not your fault: you are caught in the shift. Our culture's tumultuous influence is pulling us farther and farther away from the ancient paths set forth in Scripture—the ones that God has instilled deep within our hearts. No, you're not a perfect parent, and ROPP makes no promise to help you become one. You see, the ROPP principles are not designed for perfect parents. They don't even promise to teach anyone to raise perfect kids. Instead, ROPP encourages you to return to the ancient paths—the ones that, like the birds flying south for the winter or the squirrel burying its

over the past five weeks, and today, you will get to see a small picture of the work He has done in their lives. Continue to keep your tone positive and your focus on God as your group members follow the ancient paths that are true . . . and *rite*.

During the time since the previous session, learners practiced giving grace deposits to their spouses and children. As people enter the room, begin the process of debriefing and sharing together about the 51 Percent homework. Pray together, and remember to continue modeling deposit language as you lead the group in giving Grace Blasts, using approximately one minute per grace recipient.

nuts—have been instilled deep within us by our Creator.

Sometimes we confuse "ancient paths" with old-fashioned ways of doing things. However, "old-fashioned" can be just as unbiblical (and therefore just as wrong) as "new and innovative." Scripture encourages us that every good gift—including technology—comes from above and can be used for God's glory.

In the last exercise, you used spoken words to give grace deposits, but there are many other ways to go about this task. Think for a moment about how you could use a modern means of technology to give a grace deposit. Use the space below to briefly describe a new way to follow this ancient path (example: e-mailing a card of encouragement to a grieving friend).

No matter where you are in your family life, you recognize it. During your weeks of studying this material, you have begun learning to handle the cultural shift. You've acquired tools to help your family return to "the good way"—and begin to "walk in it."

What's *really* missing in our parenting today? The ancient paths—the ones that lead you not toward a perfect family or perfect kids, but into the step-by-step process of raising capable, responsible, self-reliant *adults*.

These confident, competent people have gone through their rites of passage. They have willingly embraced their significant tasks. They have acquired right beliefs and developed right values through properly applied logical consequences. Finally, they have moved through these essential elements securely, with abundant grace from their heavenly Father. This grace flows through their earthly parents and other designated grace depositors. They are not perfect—but they have reached true maturity because their families have followed the ancient paths.

RITE OF PASSAGE PARENTING

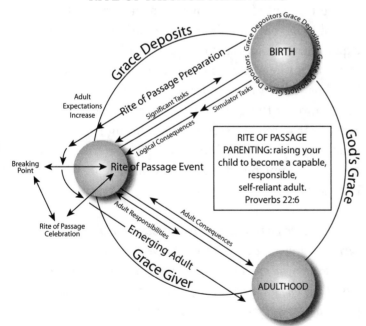

FACILITATORS: Make sure you understand the ROPP diagram before approaching this question with your group. If members seem confused, you may want to use a few moments to take a verbal hike around the ROPP circle. If you need additional help, check out the "diagram" link at www.ropparenting.com.

ROPP: After all, having children costs a lot. I don't mean the financial costs alone — I mean that you will pay a price for parenthood. You will pay the price of the time and effort it takes to develop self-reliant children. In fact, if you are not willing to pay this price as you go, you will pay it for the rest of your life. You will pay because your children will continually lean on you to raise their children, pay their bills, take care of their needs — and never become truly responsible.

This ROPP diagram shows the complete rite of passage process. Take some time to examine it now—and discuss it with your spouse or group, if you're studying the book alongside others. Take time to mark your child/children's initials on the diagram at the point you believe they've reached.

Through the pages of this workbook, I've repeatedly used the phrase *pay now, or pay later.* As parents, you can *pay now* by dealing with small concerns—or *pay later* when they become much bigger ones. *Pay now* by allowing your child to experience a rite of passage, or *pay later* when he chooses an unacceptable one like illegal drug use—or refuses to grow up and leave the shelter of your home and bank account. *Pay now* by giving your child simulator tasks, or *pay later* when she rebels against significant ones like working hard to keep a job or paying the rent for her own apartment. *Pay now* by disciplining your child, working to instruct him as he experiences the logical consequences of his actions; or *pay later* when he ends up making foolish decisions based on faulty values and beliefs. *Pay now* by pouring grace into her through thoughtful, caring words and actions; or watch her seek identity through counterfeit grace that drains her spirit account—and her life—completely dry. In fact, as my friend Tom likes to say, *pay later, pay greater.*

"Pay later, pay greater." Have you seen it in action? Write a few words on the following page about a specific situation in which you (whether purposefully or otherwise) missed out on paying a price in parenting—and ended up paying a later-but-greater price as a result.

Look back at the final ROPP diagram (page 181) and notice the many times the word "grace" appears there. That's no mistake! I urged you to "not try this at home" until we had taught you about grace deposits, ROPP's fourth essential experience, because grace, just as this diagram shows, must flow through all the ROPP essential experiences. Otherwise, you will find yourself a parent who pays both later . . . and greater.

Since grace is an integral part of the ancient paths, you can't prepare your child for a rite of passage without . . . grace. He'll try to move into adulthood on his own. You can't give your child simulator tasks leading to significant tasks without . . . grace. She'll fight you every step of the way, refusing to listen as you try to instruct her. You can't even think about giving your child logical consequences without . . . grace. The kind of law you have to lay down as you properly apply these consequences just won't work without a firm foundation—and many additional deposits—of grace.

From the time your child is born (and even before, if possible), you need to pour grace upon grace upon grace into her spirit account. In fact, your child needs to know and experience true grace

You have a choice about which kind of parent you want to be: the kind who pays now and enjoys the fruit of his labor as the children grow, or the kind who pays later and spends years trying to salvage their lives. I believe that you are the first kind of parent. Adding just one of the Rite of Passage Parenting essential experiences back into your children's lives will cost you dearly—but it will also dramatically enhance the quality of your parenting and your life together. *(Rite of Passage Parenting)* deposits from you and from other designated grace depositors (members of the grace team), or counterfeit grace (false deposits that are actually withdrawals) will pull her away every time. How do banking officials train employees to recognize counterfeit bills? You've probably heard the explanation. All new tellers spends weeks studying the real bills, memorizing their many features and acquiring such familiarity with their individual facets that the least element of error in counterfeit currency shines like a beacon into their truth-trained eyes.

You want your child to have this same experience with grace. Has he heard, seen, and experienced true grace so well and so often that he can immediately recognize its counterfeit as a false, misleading, and worthless deposit? As a Rite of Passage Parent, you must do whatever you can to make sure that grace deposits are not "what's missing" from your child's life.

Let's think again about your own kids. The auditor is paying a visit to the bank, checking the books on each child's spirit account. Which of the descriptions below sounds most like the overall evaluation? Place each of your children's initials by the description that best fits his or her spirit account.

> *a. This spirit account is overflowing. The child has had so many grace deposits that even the regular withdrawals of law in his life do not prevent him from seeing himself as God does—a wonderful creation, full of hope and promise.*
>
> *b. This spirit account's balance is positive, but not overflowing. Regular withdrawals keep threatening the total—but thoughtful deposits (often given at just the right time) have so far managed to keep it from plunging into the red.*

c. *This spirit account has zeroed out completely. Law and grace are balanced—but there is no surplus to cover the account when it suffers an upcoming withdrawal. This is scary, because as you know, that next hit could happen anytime.*

d. *Warning! Overdraft! This child's spirit account has suffered an imbalance. Someone or something (a major stress; a difficult year in school; a friend moving away) is pulling out more grace than depositors put in—and a negative balance is the result.*

e. *Red zone! This spirit account has had serious withdrawals over a long period of time, without sufficient grace deposits to balance the ledger. It is lacking the grace deposits that can move it toward a positive balance. When you see an account like this, you want to ask, "Where's the grace?"*

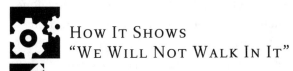

How It Shows
"We Will Not Walk In It"

Ropp By the Numbers:

81. . . percentage of young adults (ages 18–25) who count being rich among their top life goals.

10. . . percentage of young adults (ages 18–25) who count becoming more spiritual among their top life goals.[1]

55 . . . percentage of people who say that in order to achieve adulthood, you must move out of your parents' household.[2]

48 . . . percentage of 2006 college graduates who say they plan to move back into their parents' home after graduation.[3]

FACILITATORS: Choose one or more of the above statistics to discuss as time allows. You may play another "higher/lower" game if you would like, asking individuals to guess the various percentages before turning to this page in their workbooks. Facilitators who downloaded the Bible teaching segment of the Session Six ROPPcast will want to play it now. Whether or not you use this option, please study the Bible teaching in the next few paragraphs and prepare to explain or read alongside your group and/or partner.

67 . . . percentage of teens with a high sense of self (identity) whose parents recognize important rites of passage in their lives.

22 . . . percentage of teens with a high sense of self (identity) whose parents ignore important rites of passage in their lives.[4]

48 . . . percentage of teens who use instant messaging, more than twice the percentage of adults who use it.

30 . . . percentage of teens who say they can't imagine life without instant messaging.[5]

Throughout this workbook, I have pointed you toward the ancient paths . . . over and over again. In fact, I recommend that, if you have not already done so, you memorize Jeremiah 6:16 (see Fix-It #6-1 on page 202 to choose from several translations). This verse encompasses the heart of ROPP. As Rite of Passage Parents, you're standing "by the ways" that God has implanted deep within people of all cultures. You're taking the time and effort to "see." You have shown that you're willing to "ask for the ancient paths, where the good way is" and you're learning to "walk in it" step by step.

It has been my continuing prayer that God will use the ROPP material to draw you back to these ancient paths. In fact, I pray that he has already begun to lead you into good ways that will bring (as the next part of the verse describes) "rest for your souls."

I love teaching about the ancient paths, and I enjoy reminding you that you are *good* parents. I take every opportunity I can to teach parents about the cultural shift. The deep desire of my heart is to provide hope, and help, and answers that can make a lasting difference. Still, I would be less than honest if I didn't lead you to examine the final section of Jeremiah 6:16. This is the part of the verse that says, speaking of the ancient paths and good way, "But they said, 'We will not walk in it'" (Jeremiah 6:16 NASB).

Stop! Before you read any farther, write a few sentences about the meaning of the final statement of this verse. Who doesn't "walk in it"? Why don't they walk? What difference could that possibly make to you as a Rite of Passage Parent? Explore some or all of these questions and possible answers with your ROPP study partner(s).

So . . . what *does* "we will not walk in it" mean? I think you probably understand that statement better than you realize. When you were a child, did you ever disobey your parents? As an adult, have you ever done the opposite of what the authority in your life asked you to do? Do your children, even as wonderful and loving and intelligent as they are, ever go against your desires or instructions?

Your answers to those questions are the same as they were for the people Jeremiah describes. They are the same, in fact, for Adam and Eve and for every person who has lived on earth except the sinless Savior, Jesus Christ. After hearing the truth, after understanding the ancient paths, people decide to reject God's way . . . and to suffer the logical consequences of that tragic choice.

Moses understood this scenario very well. He's the guy, you may remember, chosen by God to lead his people out of hundreds of years of slavery in Egypt. In his day, he called the Israelites back to the good way of following the one true God—back to the ancient paths. We can identify with Moses because he was a lot like Peter in the New Testament. Even though he didn't always get it right, God used him in amazing ways. After Moses boldly defied Pharaoh, after he led the Israelites out of Egypt as God held back the rushing waters of the Red Sea, the Israelites willingly followed his leadership—right?

Wrong. Instead of returning to the ancient paths, instead of following their God-given authority in Moses, they kept looking back to the "good old days" of slavery in Egypt. The ultimate logical consequence for the Israelites' rebellion? Forty extra years in the desert!

Proper submission to God-given authority is a part of the ancient paths. Especially since the cultural shift, movies and other media tend to exalt those who defy authority. Can you give an example of a popular movie, television show, or book with rebellion as a central theme? Write its name here. As an alternative, write the name of a popular media star for whom rebellion seems to be a hallmark.

Even though the "first commandment with promise" (Ephesians 6:2) is to honor your father and mother, kids walk away from this ancient path every day. You've done it—I've done it—and we all know that our kids have done it. Part of becoming a Rite of Passage Parent is to recognize this trend for what it is: wrong. Disobeying the authority God has placed in your life means that you walk out from under its protection and direction—and far away from the ancient paths that God has ordained for your life.

In ROPP, I use the analogy of a building project to show parents how their influence and the cultural influence combine to shape their child's character. In this analogy, the roof of the building represents authority, held up by the rafters of grace. A graceless child begins to slide out from under his authority. This makes about as much sense as a building trying to slip away from its roof! The farther away from authority the child slides, the more vulnerable he is, and the more likely it is that his life and character will collapse.

Look at the buildings below. Place the initials of each of your children over the house that most closely resembles his current stage of construction. Remember—you're a good parent who is working to become an even better one. Let's examine and correct any construction flaws now before little flaws become . . . big problems.

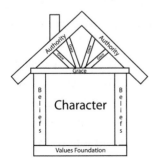
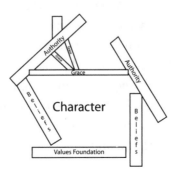
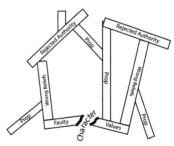

As a good parent, you also realize by now that kids are not the only ones who rebel against authority by saying, "we will not walk in it." When I travel and speak across the country, one of the hardest issues I face occurs when parents come back from the first night of a parenting conference and tell me they've done it all. They've already applied everything I've taught them and their family is now on its way to perfection. They've been there, done that, and they've got it. Yeah, yeah, yeah.

At this point, I always want to scream, "No, no, NO!" ROPP is not about perfect parents. ROPP is not about checklists and doing it all the first night, either. The heart of ROPP is . . . *relationships.* The ancient paths begin with your own relationship with God. He's the One, after all, who's making Himself at home in your life, re-hanging pictures and moving the furniture around. Please don't take the ROPP principles and make them into a checklist, a rule book, or something you can fix overnight. Instead, take them back to the place where they began. Kneel before the Lord with your family on your heart and your open Bible beside you. Ask Him where to start—one step at a time.

I like to tell parents that *a changed life changes lives.* The only way to begin making changes—any changes—in your family is to allow God to change you. Where do you need to change? Do you need to go back and ask your own parents to pronounce you an adult? Do you need to start giving your kids simulator tasks that build toward significant tasks? Maybe you've just begun to recognize that you have not been a grace depositor for your child. You need to spend time giving grace day after day and month after month before you begin to think of adding logical consequences to his life. Where does God want to make changes in your life as a parent? That's the heart of "how it shows" in you and in your family.

MOMSPEAK: *Sometimes, I can be a very slow learner. Like the children of Israel, sometimes I need a few laps around the desert before I understand that God wants to "fix it" . . . in me.*

I understood, or thought I understood, what my writing partner meant when he told me, over and over again, "a changed life changes lives." God has blessed me with the privilege of listening to and learning the ROPP principles so that I could assist Walker in translating them into print. Even before I began working with him, our two oldest daughters traveled overseas with Awe Star Ministries. My husband, Tom, and I were amazed at the ways God transformed them in some of the very ways we've studied in this workbook.

What I did not recognize immediately, however, was that God also wanted to change . . . me. I'm the kind of mom, like many of you, who tries to do things right—but sometimes, my kids still do things wrong. Tom and I have two college-age daughters and three children still at home. We're walking through the essential experiences every day. In our life—and in our friends' lives—we see the hurt caused when we stray from God's ancient paths. The cultural shift has certainly hit home in the Pieper home— over and over again.

ROPP has brought me some answers for the questions I had as a newlywed—as a young mom—and even today. I love to tell people about these answers, and about the four ROPP essential experiences. What I tell them first, however, is neither one of these things. What I tell them first is that a changed life changes lives.

As a mom who wants to get it right, I have to be willing

to allow God to make Himself at home—to change my life. I have to be willing each day to lay down all of my rights and ask God to extend His grace to me. I have to be willing to allow my children to grow up, and, at the right time, to experience a rite of passage event. I have to be willing to "pay now" by taking the time and trouble to give my children simulator, then significant tasks—even when it might seem easier to do things myself. I have to be willing to be a grace depositor for my family members and others, whether or not I think they deserve it. Most of all, I have to be willing to submit to God's loving authority as He fills me with His grace. He lovingly allows me to act as a capable, responsible, self-reliant adult who is choosing, day after day after day, to walk out these truths.

A changed life changes lives. *I believe this because one of those changed lives is . . . me!*

DadSpeak: *I've mentioned my two sons, Jeremiah and Caleb, several times in this book. If you've read ROPP, you know about the ways God has worked— even through a dad who doesn't always get it right— to touch the lives of two very different young men.*

One of the questions parents ask me as I travel is the question I asked myself when I looked at organized, efficient Jeremiah and his loveable, irrepressible brother who always seems to have to learn . . . the hard way. (Actually, Caleb, like Jesus, calls it "the narrow way." That's the New Testament term for what I've been calling "the ancient paths".)

So, how do you use ROPP to meet the needs of a Jeremiah—and a Caleb? I've had parents ask me how to "fix it" for all sorts of kids with all different kinds of temperaments and all kinds of family backgrounds. It sounds impossible, doesn't it? How could one parenting plan fit so many different personalities, learning styles, and abilities or disabilities?

The reason ROPP *works is that it's not a new plan—instead, it's part of the ancient paths that God has placed within every individual from the dawn of creation. Man, as a created being, finds his true fulfillment only when he is in sync with his Creator. When you introduce a child to the* ROPP *essential experiences, you're meeting his deepest needs and longings. That's true whether he's laidback, strong-willed, dyslexic, hearing-impaired, or the winner of the next Nobel Prize.* ROPP *works for all different kinds of kids from all different kinds of families because* ROPP *begins and ends with a relationship with the Creator—the One who designed the ancient paths. We've given you FIX-ITs in this workbook to help you customize* ROPP *for yourself and your family. But the only One who can really "fix it" is the One who makes Himself at home . . . in you.*

Through your study of the ROPP Workbook, God has undoubtedly shown you some areas where He wants to make Himself at home. Whether you're remodeling your home or your family, some areas need more urgent attention than others. Circle the essential experience below that you believe needs the most immediate Fix-It. As time allows, explain why you think this is true.

Rite of Passage

Significant Tasks

Logical Consequences

Grace Deposits

FACILITATORS: Throughout this workbook, I've emphasized that the best way you can help your group members is to model open, honest, and humble communication. We all have areas of need—areas of invitation for God to make Himself at home by changing us. Take a moment to stop and pray aloud for the group here, asking God to take the ROPP principles and apply them to each individual and each family. Make sure to keep this a positive and encouraging time in which you remind these good parents that He's already working to make them even better ones.

ROPP: When I teach, I often have people ask me, "Walker, do you *always* practice what you preach? Did you *always* give your kids logical consequences? Did you *always* offer them significant tasks? And grace deposits—did you offer those at every single opportunity?"

Once again, you know the answer. My wife and sons would be the first to tell you that I am far from the perfect parent. One of the great things about Rite of Passage Parenting is that you only have to institute its principles 51 percent of the time. I tell people that kids are great mathematicians. If you have any doubt about that, watch what happens when you try splitting a candy bar between three of them.

Your kids will know whether you apply significant tasks, or logical consequences, or grace deposits *more often than not.* That's 51 percent of the time. *Rite of Passage Parenting* covers and contains all of

Rite of Passage Parenting celebration "You Will Find Rest for Your Souls"

Do you remember the deposit language taught in Session Five? The fourth step in that teaching was "just do it." You know by now that grace deposits are not just what you *say;* they're also what you *do.*

By now, I think you also know that *all* the ROPP principles are much more than what you say. They're what you do—and, more importantly, what you allow God to do through your life. Acts 1:1 says that "Jesus began both to *do* and to teach." He not only taught great truths—He lived them. Living them, or *doing it* is important, because studying the ancient paths won't do you or your family a bit of good unless you surrender to walk in them. As you do, God will give you the "rest for your souls" that He promises. You will be most fulfilled, most at peace, most able to *rest* when you're walking His ancient paths because they represent the way He designed you to live in the first place. When you follow the ancient paths, you're following . . . Him.

It's time to celebrate the good work God has done in you and in your family! Take this time to write down two statements that on the following page briefly describe ways God has brought you closer to His ancient paths as a result of studying this workbook. Please make these as specific as possible, for example: "I learned that I need to give my child a balance of law and grace, or she will plunge deeper into rebellion" or "I realized that I have never given my older teen the benefit of a true rite of passage, so he keeps trying out counterfeit ones."

these events—but if you had looked into the Moore house while Caleb and Jeremiah still lived at home, you would not have seen it operating perfectly twenty-four hours a day, seven days a week. We are far from perfect . . . but . . . we serve a perfect God who can help us go beyond ourselves to reflect His grace. *(Rite of Passage Parenting)*

FACILITATORS: I've designed this segment of the session as a meaningful time for you and for your partner or group. Keep your tone positive to emphasize the fact that the group is celebrating God's work in their lives while moving forward into the "good plans" He has for them in the future. Ask God to give you grace as you extend grace deposits to them and as the group moves toward signing the ROPP Covenant, FIX-IT #6-2 on page 20.

We all bring certain expectations to the study of a book like this. I've tried to make mine clear throughout our time together by listing them in the "goals" section of each session. However, I think you know by now that I'm a fellow struggler. God is always teaching me something new—and I love to share those things with other good parents. Often, He surprises me by teaching me something I never expected to learn, or doing something I never anticipated. Scripture says that He is "able to do exceedingly abundantly above all that we ask or think" (Ephesians 3:20). Those are the kind of surprises I love!

FACILITATORS: This time should be serious but also sensitive. The hopes/prayer requests that learners share aloud may bring tears, since ancient paths reflect our deepest longings. Acknowledge the importance of this time by modeling attentiveness to each request. If possible, write the "Hopes" list on a white board as each person speaks. When the last person has finished sharing, take time to pray for each request. You may want to encourage "popcorn" prayer in which each participant prays a sentence or two about a request, then another does the same for another request until every request has been lifted up at least once.

Now, we want to celebrate the ways God has surprised you through this study. Did you understand something you had never thought about before? Did a Bible verse come alive for you, or did you learn something new about yourself or your kids? Write down a surprise or two here (please write something different than the "ancient paths" learning you listed in the previous question) and be ready to share it with your spouse, if possible, and/or group.

God intends to use our lives as His instruments of blessing. As He changes us, our lives touch and change those around us. That includes, first of all, our families. God's ancient paths for the family include words and actions that demonstrate mutual love, honor, and respect. These ancient paths also include growth toward maturity, meaningful work, and the building of values that line up with His will and Word—sealed and secured by authority and the constant flow of appropriate grace.

As you've learned, the cultural shift has often led us away from those ancient paths, often without our realizing it. Thankfully, God's work extends beyond culture and family problems, beyond technology and shifting patterns in music or media. He tells us, "'I have good plans for you, not plans to hurt you. I will give you hope and a good future'" (Jeremiah 29:11b NCV). He has designed these plans (you guessed it) to help you return to His ancient paths!

Ancient paths. You've heard about them from beginning to end of this study. The ancient paths give us hope for the future because we know that by following them, we're returning to God's original design. In the midst of a changing culture, hope for the future is definitely . . . something to celebrate.

What hopes has God awakened in your heart as you've begun to reexamine His ancient paths? Take the time now to write a short sentence that describes one specific hope, then share it with your spouse or group, if possible, as a prayer request. Examples: "I hope that my children will gain self-reliance in the area of finances." "I hope that my child will learn to share my values in the area of sexuality."

I'm so thankful that God included families in His ancient paths. They're a beautiful, essential means of carrying out His purposes. However, you also know that His work extends far beyond the family. Right now, I'd like to ask you a question: Have you ever noticed all the "one anothers" in Scripture? We are to "love one another" (John 13:34; 15:12, 17); "serve one another" (Galatians 5:13); "pray for one another"

FACILITATORS: Turn to FIX-IT #6-2, page 203. If you wish, you may prepare in advance by copying this covenant onto blank paper, or downloading and printing it from the **www.ropparenting.com** Web site. This way, no one has to remove a sheet from his or her book.

Read, or have a member read, the Rite of Passage Parenting Covenant aloud. During a few moments of silence, ask each member to pray about surrendering his or her heart and life not to ROPP, but to Jesus—and to *one another*.

When an Awe Star team is ready to go into a new assignment together, we "pull it in." We stand in a circle, and everyone extends one hand toward the center of the group so that all hands are on top of . . . that's right, *one another*. We then pray and, in the process, surrender ourselves to the will of God and to holding *one another* accountable. I

(James 5:16); "bear with one another in love" (Ephesians 4:2); and "forgiv[e] one another" (Ephesians 4:32), to name only a few.

If you're studying this workbook as part of a group, you have lived out these "one anothers" and more as you have come together every week. You have shared honestly about your parenting and your children. You have prayed together. I hope that you have laughed together, and I imagine you may even have cried together a time or two or . . . more.

I'll say it again: times have changed. The culture has shifted, and many parents and children today lack the nurturing support of intergenerational bonds. One of the ways God has provided to "fix it" for our culture is the strong fellowship of other believers who can act when our extended family cannot, will not, or simply does not know how. We discussed that idea in Session Five when we learned about designated grace depositors.

At the beginning of this workbook, you signed a ROPP Parenting Contract. I'd like you to lay that aside now in favor of a new one. As a part of it, the members of your group will surrender to practicing the "one anothers" we all need so desperately. Why do we need them? Because, once again, the "one anothers" all reflect His ancient paths in our lives—the ones God has designed us to walk in from before the foundations of time.

When you have a question, you now have a group of people committed to *help one another* find answers. When you have a concern, you now have a group of people surrendered to *pray for one another* . . . as you just finished doing. When you stumble and fall, you have people who will stand beside you, willing to *forgive one another*. When you need a grace deposit—or a bunch of them—you now have a group of people who know how to give them to you—and are surrendered and ready to *encourage one another.*

My friends and family all know that I carry around an old Bible. I dearly love it, because it's been my companion for a long time. As you might guess, it's well-worn, filled with markings, underlinings, and words that I've written in the margins. Its pages remind me daily of the way God has worked and of the good plans He has for me and for those I love. This Bible, in fact, is the one God used to point toward the ancient paths expressed in ROPP.

I would never ask you to replace your Bible with this workbook. Instead, I'd love to see you use the workbook right alongside your Bible, and let them both become tattered, torn, and well-used. Read and reread them alongside *Rite of Passage Parenting.* Go back over the workbook questions and answers. Write notes in the margins—and *pray.* Pray for your spouse, your children, and your fellow group members. Please know that both my writing partner, Marti, and I are praying for you too. We're asking God to use this material, and to use *you,* to teach and train and raise, not children, but capable, responsible, self-reliant . . . adults. That's an ancient path worth . . . celebrating!

 51 PERCENT:

1. Although you don't have regular homework this time, when you go home, I want you to do something special. Of course, I want you to pray and read your Bible. I want you to practice the ROPP principles. But I have one more special request. It involves what you told me when you bought this workbook—the one where you said, in effect, *make yourself at home.* In this

recommend that, as the Facilitator, you lead the group in prayer and begin calling forth what you have cast into them all along: they are good parents who want to support one another in the lifelong process of becoming even better parents—Rite of Passage Parents.

Ask God to help you make this a memorable time. I've deliberately kept this session short to allow plenty of open-ended sharing time. Use it as a milestone marker—and watch expectantly to see how God uses it!

FACILITATORS: As the group exits today, you may want to cast the vision for an upcoming ROPP Reunion. Encourage members to go through the final set of ROPP Devotions and to do the 51 Percent homework for this session, including Fix-It #6-3, the ROPP Testimony. Invite them to return for a ROPP Reunion in four to six weeks. At this time, you will lead members in sharing their testimonies, praying together, and encouraging one another in ways you've already experienced through the fellowship of this group. If you wish, you may download specific plans for this ROPP Reunion in the Facilitators' section of www.ropparenting.com.

case, I want to make myself at home in a place that I consider sacred: the refrigerator door.

For many families, the refrigerator door has become a family message center (see ROPP Devotional, p. 27). Now that our boys are grown, ours is not nearly as interesting as it used to be—but even though we're missing the school calendars and sports schedules, Cathy and I leave notes for one another in that same spot. The refrigerator reminds me of things I consider very important. May I make myself at home with yours?

I want you to take Fix-It #6-2 on page 203 and post it right there on your refrigerator door, or another special place where you'll see it—and reread it—often. You're more likely to remember the "one anothers" if you see them day after day after day. If you'd like, whenever you pass by this Fix-It, pray for . . . one another. Ask God to "fix it" for their families and for yours. See if He reminds you to give another member—or your Facilitator—a grace deposit by calling him or sending her a note. Maybe, instead, He wants you to call and ask another member to pray for you and your family. Whatever you do, don't leave that Fix-It in the back of your book and ignore it. Allow God to continue to *fix it*, right there from the vantage point of . . . the refrigerator door.

■ 2. WHAT ARE THE ODDS? In this section of each workbook chapter, I've provided you with stories of people who have seen God do amazing things as they applied the ROPP principles. This time, it's your turn! In Fix-It #6-3, on page 204 you will find a simple template to use in preparing your own ROPP testimony. I encourage you to work through these ideas and prepare to share your story with your fellow group members (see your Facilitator for information about an upcoming ROPP Reunion) and other good parents you meet. They're the ones who want to become even better parents by learning about ROPP, and learning to raise not just children, but capable, responsible, self-reliant . . . adults.

3. Over a five-day period, read and study the five-day ROPP Devotion Guide that follows the Fix-Its for this session.

⚙ fix-it #6-1: Jeremiah 6:16, Versions to Choose From for Memorization

Thus says the LORD, "Stand by the ways and see and ask for the ancient paths, Where the good way is, and walk in it; And you will find rest for your souls. But they said, 'We will not walk in it'" (NASB).

This is what the Lord says: "Stand where the roads cross and look. Ask where the old way is, where the good way is, and walk on it. If you do, you will find rest for yourselves. But they have said, 'We will not walk on the good way'" (NCV).

Thus says the LORD: "Stand in the ways and see, And ask for the old paths, where the good way is, And walk in it; Then you will find rest for your souls. But they said, 'We will not walk in it'" (NKJV).

God's Message yet again: "Go stand at the crossroads and look around. Ask for directions to the old road, The tried-and-true road. Then take it. Discover the right route for your souls. But they said, 'Nothing doing. We aren't going that way.' I even provided watchmen for them to warn them, to set off the alarm. But the people said, 'It's a false alarm. It doesn't concern us'" (MSG).

This is what the LORD says: "Stand at the crossroads and look; ask for the ancient paths, ask where the good way is, and walk in it, and you will find rest for your souls. But you said, 'We will not walk in it'" (NIV).

FIX-IT #6-2:
RITE OF PASSAGE PARENTING COVENANT

Thus says the Lord, "Stand by the ways and see and ask for the ancient paths, Where the good way is, and walk in it; And you will find rest for your souls" (Jeremiah 6:16 NASB).

I AM A RITE OF PASSAGE PARENT. I care about my children, and I want to help them face the challenges of our changing culture. I know I can become an even better parent by returning to the "ancient paths" that God has designed and instilled within me as a beloved part of His creation. I know that, along the way, I will need encouragement, support, and prayer from fellow Rite of Passage Parents standing alongside me.

THEREFORE, believing that God has created me with both the deep desire and ability to become a Rite of Passage Parent, I surrender my life to the ancient path of raising capable, responsible, self-reliant adults. I will prayerfully and appropriately apply the ROPP principles at least 51 percent of the time. I hold myself accountable before the Lord and before my covenant partners. I will pray for these partners, extend grace deposits to them, and pray for them regularly.

(signed) _____ (participant)

_____

_____

_____

_____

_____

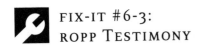

FIX-IT #6-3:
ROPP TESTIMONY

ROPP SUMMARY: Before our Awe Star student missionaries go overseas, we train them to share their testimonies, firsthand accounts of God's work in their lives. Scripture encourages us to proclaim to others what we have "seen and heard" (1 John 1:3). As a Rite of Passage Parent, you also have a testimony . . . of God's work through the ROPP principles. Use the guidelines and outline below to help you share wisely and effectively.

GUIDELINES: Keep your testimony (1) **Brief**: share one principle and related experience at a time. (2) **Interesting**: use vivid language that communicates how you felt and what you experienced. (3) **God-centered**: focus on God's work rather than your own weaknesses or strengths.

OUTLINE: Follow a simple, three-point outline when you prepare your ROPP testimony. Use the space following each outline point to fill in your own story.

1. **My life before ROPP**: What parenting struggles did I have? Can I share these in a way that relates specifically to others that I know are present?

2. **A ROPP teaching that applied to me**: What was the specific ROPP principle that touched my life? How did I personally apply it to my parenting?

3. **My life since ROPP**: How did God use this principle to change me? How did He use it to make a difference in the life of my child? How is He using it to change my family today?

ROPP SURRENDER: As a Rite of Passage Parent, I believe that *a changed life changes lives*. Because of this, I surrender to sharing my ROPP testimony with others.

RITE OF PASSAGE PARENTING
DEVOTION GUIDE

DAY ONE: WALLET-ECTOMY

READING: *Create in me a clean heart, O God, And renew a steadfast spirit within me* (Psalm 51:10).

OBSERVATION: Every time I turn around, someone is giving me another card to carry. My grocery store offers a discount card, Blockbuster wants me to have its membership card, and recently, Delta gave me a medallion card to prove that I am a frequent flier.

My wallet used to be a thin, anemic little thing. It held my driver's license, a picture of my wife and, on a good day, three bucks. It seems that as I have grown thicker, so has my wallet. Now, when I carry it in my hip pocket, it looks as though I have a growth on my posterior—definitely the last place I need any additional bulk. If I reduced my wallet size, I'm sure I could drop two pants' sizes.

I examined my wallet today and discovered an AAA card that I have carried since 1984 but only used twice. I found my health insurance card and a separate prescription card that works about as well as my Walgreen's credit card. I also found two American Express cards, one personal and one business; and two Visa cards, one personal and one business. In addition, I found a class C driver's license and a Sam's Wholesale membership card. (Now, this comes in handy. If the disciples had owned a Sam's card, they wouldn't have wondered where to get food to feed five thousand people.) My wallet also holds a MasterCard, a phone card, a credit union card, more airline cards, about a half dozen receipts from who knows where, a picture of my wife and sons and . . . the same three bucks.

What I really need is to perform a "wallet-ectomy." I need to determine what is truly important, and just carry the other stuff as needed. However, I have trouble telling the important and the semi-important apart.

Sometimes I have the same problem when it comes to my children. My work provides them the necessities of life, but allowing them to do without some things would free me to spend a little more time with them. Which is more important? Maybe my life, like my wallet, carries too many nonesssentials. Maybe Dr. Jesus needs to do a "heart-ectomy" on me while I am operating on my wallet.

PRINCIPLE: Parents who know how to prioritize will not live in regret.

PRAYER: *Dear Father, help me learn the difference between the urgent and the important. Today, help me apply my energy toward people and events that will have eternal impact. Father, I realize there is nothing else on earth so important as my family. Help me to rearrange my schedule so that the true priorities come first. Amen.*

DAY TWO: CHEAP AIRFARE

READING: *Look at the birds of the air, for they neither sow nor reap nor gather into barns; yet your heavenly Father feeds them. Are you not of more value than they?* (Matthew 6:26).

OBSERVATION: Over the past few years, the entire airline industry has had to make changes. But what about those companies that have had trouble stepping up their standards? As a very frequent flier, I know all the signs. You can tell you are using a cheap airline when: (1) You do not purchase a "ticket" but a "chance." (2) Every insurance machine in the terminal is sold out. (3) Before the flight, the passengers get together to elect a pilot. (4) You cannot board the plane without having exact change. (5) Finally, you know you are on a cheap airline when all the planes have both a restroom and. . . a chapel.

Recently, as I was boarding a plane, the flight attendants announced that the plane was experiencing mechanical difficulties, so we would need to change equipment. (They should just say, "Folks, this plane is broken. We will have to move you to another plane and hope that it will fly.")

Out came the next piece of "equipment": a very small prop plane to replace the brand-new jet we had just boarded. This plane looked as though it had not flown in years. The only thing holding it together was its spotty, rust-streaked coat of paint, and it had a flat tire. Thankfully, the flight attendant said we would be on our way as soon as they aired up the flat.

With the airplane loaded and the doors closed, the flight attendant began to go through the safety procedures—until the pilot paged her. This tiny plane was overloaded, so someone would have to change to another flight. One lucky volunteer left. Again, the door closed, and the flight attendant began her spiel when we heard "Urrrrrh, urrrrh, urrrh, urh." This time, the engine would not start.

The door opened once more to allow a mechanic to board. For forty minutes, all we heard was the "urrrrh, urh, urrh" sound. At one point, the mechanic yelled,

"I think I got the backup batteries working." Now, that phrase is the last thing I want to hear from an airplane mechanic! I want him to *know* that he has fixed whatever was wrong. Finally, the plane took off, and I spent the entire flight in prayer. Sometimes, a bargain ticket comes at a very high price.

PRINCIPLE: Pay now, or pay later. You do not want either an airplane or your parenting to . . . crash.

PRAYER: *Dear Father, I do not want my parenting to cause my children's lives to crash or burn. Help me take the time to help them become ready to leave the nest. Through Your wisdom, may I release them to fly! Amen.*

DAY THREE: GENERIC MAN

READING: *The poor shall eat and be satisfied; Those who seek Him will praise the* LORD. *Let your heart live forever!* (Psalm 22:26).

OBSERVATION: I have come to the conclusion that I, Walker Moore, have a blessed life. In fact, when people ask me, "How are you doing?" I answer back, "I am suffering from satisfaction!"

I am married to an absolutely gorgeous, smart, and multitalented wife. I am blessed with two sons and a daughter-in-love who are the joy of my life. I am blessed to have a wonderful job and a tremendous staff. And I am grateful to God that I have always been able to go . . . generic.

You see, my family does not use generic products. My wife uses expensive shampoo, sold only at the beauty shop. Next to her exotic brand sits mine . . . "Big Blue Dandruff Shampoo." She has specialized hairspray, and I have "Stuff That Plasters Your Hair to Your Head," guaranteed to hold every strand in place during a Category Five hurricane. My sons can only wear designer cologne. For Christmas, they want Polo or Cool Water, but I am so blessed that they give me something called . . . "Tester." The only jeans that fit their bodies are found at American Eagle or Old Navy. I am so blessed. My brand is sold especially at outlet malls: "Irregular."

Even in sickness, my family requires the big names like Sudafed or Benadryl. Not me! My medicine comes in a plain white box with large black letters reading, "Tiny Red Tablets for People with Big Noses" or "Bottle of Red Liquid to Guzzle So You'll Feel Drowsy." Who needs Diet Coke? Instead, I choose the real man's drink, "Buy-Rite Cola"—equally good, sometimes carbonated.

There is only one problem in being a generic man. When I actually wear a designer brand, it looks . . . generic. You can give me a $500 suit, but I guarantee that once it hits my body, it will look as though it came from Woolworth's. People say that clothes make the man, but I have to disagree. I make the clothes . . . look cheap.

I am so glad that when God decided to save the world, He did not send a generic savior. He sent us the very best. When I accepted Jesus as my Lord and Savior, He did not make my life generic and ordinary. Instead, He says I am a Designer original, a person that He knew before the foundation of the world. He has called me to be His child—the child of a King. I am truly blessed.

PRINCIPLE: If you want your child to live a blessed life, teach him or her to be satisfied with generic things and find total fulfillment in . . . a designer Savior.

PRAYER: *Dear Father, in You, I find real satisfaction. I know that Satan offers subtle substitutes with empty promises. Help my child see that You are the best, and that the world's offers do not even compare. Amen.*

DAY FOUR: SUBTLE SIGNS

READING: *Correct your son, and he will give you rest; Yes, he will give delight to your soul* (Proverbs 29:17).

OBSERVATION: Families today are in trouble. I am talking about serious trouble. As I listen to parents pour out their hearts, I wonder why they did not see the trouble coming. It reminds me of people who were hit by a train—surely they saw or heard the whistle in the distance? The difficulty lies in the fact that most people do not recognize the danger signs of an unhealthy family. If your family displays any one of the following symptoms, you may be headed for disaster:

- Most conversations with your children begin with, "Put the gun down, and then we can talk."
- Most of your family disputes can be seen at three o'clock on "Family Court."
- You are trying to get your four-year-old to switch to decaf.
- The school principal keeps your work number on his speed-dial.
- A police officer knocks on your door wondering if everything is all right, since he has not heard from you yet that day.

- Your family pet is hooked on Prozac.
- People have trouble understanding your children, who learned to speak through clenched teeth.
- When you want to talk with your children, they check their Palm Pilots first.
- Your child's pager continually goes off after midnight.
- Every T-shirt your daughter owns has something to do with . . . wrestling.

In more than thirty years of working with families in crisis, I have discovered a common theme: they waited too long to deal with their problems. Crisis, in most families, does not happen overnight. The issues have grown and developed over the years, but the parents have ignored them. The longer you wait, the more difficult the problems are to correct.

I am a typical male: I hate asking for directions. I have to get way off course before I stop and ask anyone how to get back on the right road. All along, my wife is asking me to pull over and get some help. The longer I wait, the more difficult it is for me to get myself and my family back on track.

A minor, more gentle correction is always easier to make than a major one. Most problems our teenagers experience begin during their childhood years. Handle issues of concern as early as possible. God will give you the wisdom if you ask for help and direction.

PRINCIPLE: Pride is the tool the Enemy uses to convince us to avoid admitting—or resolving—conflicts. Remember, if you pay later, you pay . . . *greater.*

PRAYER: *Dear Father, many times I have just ignored a difficult issue in my child's life, hoping it would go away. Instead, the problem has grown. Now, instead of dealing with a little issue, we are facing a major crisis. I ask for a bigger portion of grace just to get back on the right road. Thank You for forgiving me. Amen.*

DAY FIVE: IF ONLY

READING: *Bless the LORD, O my soul; And all that is within me, bless His holy name! Bless the LORD, O my soul, And forget not all His benefits: Who forgives all your iniquities, Who heals all your diseases, Who redeems your life from destruction, Who crowns you with lovingkindness and tender mercies, Who satisfies your mouth with good things, So that your youth is renewed like the eagle's* (Psalm 103:1–5).

OBSERVATION: Each day, I am increasingly aware that this journey on earth is, at most, short. I wonder if Methuselah ever stood, staring into the mirror after living for 969 years, thinking . . . "Where did the time go?" I can imagine him holding one of his great-great-great-great-great-grandchildren on his knee and reminiscing," . . . seems only like yesterday I celebrated my five hundredth birthday." I wonder if he had any regrets—if he ever said, "If only . . ."

The farther I get on this journey, the more clearly I can look back upon the things I have left in the wake of my life. What I fear most is that I might see . . . "if only." "If only" are those missed opportunities that come back to haunt you. They assume many shapes and forms. "If only I had risked that job change, my life would have taken a different direction," or "If only I had said 'I'm sorry,' I wouldn't have had that broken relationship." "If only I hadn't worked so hard and had spent more time with my children, they might have different lives today."

I like the cleaning solution "Formula 409". Not only is it a great product, but the way it got its name fascinates me. Do you know the story? On the four hundred ninth attempt, the scientists finally succeeded in developing what they wanted. What might have happened if on the four hundred eighth try, they had decided to give up? They might still be saying, "If only."

I wonder how many of you moms and dads and grandmas and grandpas go to bed at night feeling like . . . failures? I wonder how many of you have said, "If only I had done it differently"? I wonder how many people's regrets have crippled them from being all that God designed them to be. The good news is that our God has all power and authority over your "If only." Even better, "if only" you will commit your yesterdays to Him, He will turn them into today's victories.

Our God is the God of today and yesterday and tomorrow. His resurrection power helps us face "if only," the mistakes and failures of the past. This is the compelling message that the Marys brought to the apostle Peter. How many times did he fail? How many times did he sit, head in his hands, muttering, "If only I hadn't denied Him"? And yet, from the empty tomb, the angel spoke to the Marys: "Go tell the disciples and . . . *Peter* to come back."

PRINCIPLE: God is a God of the second and third and thousandth chance. He will redeem the "If only" . . . if only you will let Him.

PRAYER: *Dear Father, I thank You for the journey that You have led me through for the past six weeks. Your Words have become my light and life. I do not want to be like those in Jeremiah's day who said, "We will not walk in it."*

I say "yes" to Your ancient paths and yield my ways to become Your ways. I want to be used as a tool of righteousness to instill Your purposes in my children's lives. I thank You that You have never abandoned my family. I pray that You will be glorified in everything we say and do. Again, thank You for showing me Your ancient paths and teaching me to become a Rite of Passage Parent. Amen.

NOTES

SESSION ONE—MAKE YOURSELF AT HOME

1. Tovia Smith, "Technology Lets Parents Track Kids' Every Move," http://www.npr.org/templates/story/story.php?storyId=5725196 , viewed 8/30/06.
2. Barna Research Institute, "Most Twentysomethings Put Christianity on the Shelf Following Spiritually Active Teen Years," http://www.barna.org/FlexPage.aspx?Page=BarnaUpdateNarrowPreview&BarnaUpdateID=245 , viewed 9/5/06.
3. Shampa Mazumdar, "Kinkeeping and Caregiving: Contributions of Older People in Immigrant Families," Journal of Comparative Family Studies (January 1, 2004). Archived at: http://www.highbeam.com/library/doc3.asp?docid=1G1:113302756
4. Barbar Kantrowitz and Peg Tyrie, "The Fine Art of Letting Go," *Newsweek* (May 22, 2006), 56.
5. Ibid.
6. John David Rook, MS, LPC, NCC; e-mail correspondence, 12/14/06.
7. http://darwinawards.com/darwin/, viewed 1/27/07.

SESSION TWO—RITE OF PASSAGE

1. Thomas Hine, *The Rise and Fall of the American Teenager* (New York: Avon Books, 1999), 4.
2. "Timeline for Inventing Entertainment: The Motion Pictures and Sound Recordings of the Edison Companies," http://memory.loc.gov/ammem/edhtml/edtime.html, viewed 1/29/07.
3. "George Washington Lives!—on the Internet!," http://www.education-world.com/a_lesson/lesson051.shtml, viewed 1/29/07.
4. "John Quincy Adams," www.ipl.org/div/potus/jqadams.html, viewed 1/29/07.
5. "Timeline for Pocahontas 1595–1617," http://www.educationalsynthesis.org/famamer/Pocahontas/Poca-timeline.html, viewed 1/29/07.
6. Rachel Salman, "Wolfgang Amadeus Mozart," http://www.incwell.com/Biographies/Mozart.html, viewed 1/29/07.
7. Adapted from Ronald Koteskey, *Understanding Adolescence* (Wheaton, Illinois: Victor Books, 1987), 20.
8. Ronald Koteskey, *Understanding Adolescence* (Wheaton, Illinois: Victor Books, 1987; revised electronic edition, Koteskey, 2005), 7–8.
9. Pamela Paul, "The Permaparent Trap," *Psychology Today* (September–October 2003), 42.
10. "FastFacts: Demographics/Family Life," The Network on Transitions to Adulthood, www.transad.pop.upenn.edu/media/facts_bd.htm, viewed 12/11/06.
11. Brent Higgins, personal interview, 12/13/06.
12. Paul, "The Permaparent Trap," 45.

SESSION THREE—SIGNIFICANT TASKS

1. "K-State Professor Links Rise in Costs of Raising Children to Changes in Lifestyle," http://www.mediarelations.k-state.edu/WEB/News/NewsReleases/raisingcost110204.html, viewed 10/9/06.
2. Kantrowitz and Tyrie, "Letting Go," 56.

3. "Fast Facts: Work and Education," www.transad.pop.upenn.edu/media/facts_wa.htm, viewed 1/1/07. (the network on transitions to adulthood)

4. LiveScience Staff, "Why Teens Are Lousy at Chores," www.livescience.com/humanbiology/050517_teen_thought.html, viewed 1/1/07.

5. Tammy Layman, e-mail correspondence, 1/11/07.

SESSION FOUR—LOGICAL CONSEQUENCES

1. "Mom Auctions Off Family's Mess on eBay," www.nbc4.tv/family/5611507/detail.html, viewed 1/4/07.

2. "Tardy Parents Get Sent to Detention," www.sciencedaily.com/upi/index.php?feed=Quirks&article=UPI-1-20061001-20035300-bc-us-tardy.xml, viewed 10/12/06.

3. "Parents Who Host Lose the Most," www.nhtsa.dot.gov/PEOPLE/INJURY/alcohol/StopImpaired/planners/2311_ParentYouthPlanner/pages/OpEd.htm, viewed 1/4/07.

4. Margaret Feinberg, "Generation Debt: Why Money Is Such a Big Issue," www.churchplantingvillage.net/site/apps/nl/content2.asp?c=iiJTKZPEJpH&b=849683&ct=1722599, viewed 1/4/07.

5. Kantrowitz and Tyrie, "Letting Go," 53.

6. H. Stephen Glenn and Jane Nelsen, *Raising Self-Reliant Children in a Self-Indulgent World: Seven Building Blocks for Raising Capable Young People* (Roseville, California: Prima Publishing, 2000), 67.

7. Tom Pieper, personal interview, 11/29/07.

8. Josh McDowell, *Why Wait: What You Need to Know about the Teen Sexuality Crisis* (San Bernadino, California: Here's Life Publishers, 1989), 79.

SESSION FIVE—GRACE DEPOSITS

1. "Bulletproofing Our Schools—with Faith," www.family.org/faith/A000000904.cfm, accessed 1//8/07.

2. Fred A. Hartley III, *Parenting at its Best: How to Raise Children with a Passion for Life* (Grand Rapids, MI: Fleming H. Revell, 2003), 165.

3. "Grandparents—Demographics and Roles," http://www.pobronson.com/factbook/pages/95.html, viewed 1/30/07.

4. Betty Beale, "The Roles of Grandparents in Educating Today's Children," http://www.highbeam.com/doc/1G1-112686167.html, from *Journal of Instructional Psychology* (Dec. 1, 2003), accessed 1/13/07.

5. Peggy Nunley, e-mail correspondence; 1/11/07, 1/16/07.

SESSION SIX—RITE OF PASSAGE PARENTING CELEBRATION

1. Sharon Jayson, "GenNext's Goals, Problems" http://www.usatoday.com/news/nation/2007-01-09-views_x.htm?POE=click-refer, viewed 1/9/07

2. Kantrowitz and Tyrie, "Letting Go," 62.

3. Ibid., 56.

4. "Teens Report: Parental Inattention to Their Important 'Rites of Passage' Has High Price Tag," http://www.sadd.org/teenstoday/rites.htm, viewed 1/20/07.

5. Will Lester, "Poll: 'IM-ing' Divides Teens, Adults," http://www.siliconvalley.com/mld/siliconvalley/business/technology/16187478.htm, viewed 1/21/07.

www.ropparenting.com

You're a good parent who cares about your kids, so I encourage you to visit the *Rite of Passage Parenting* (ROPP) Web site where you'll find a variety of tools to guide you as a Rite of Passage Parent.

▸▸ **ROPP MEMBERSHIP:** access to supplemental ROPP materials, free of charge.

▸▸ **ROPP STORE:** the *rite* place to order additional books, other ROPP materials, and the *Rite of Passage Parenting Workbook* (Thomas Nelson, 2007) designed to help you personalize ROPP and *fix it* for your own family. Recommended for a small group setting, the *Rite of Passage Parenting Workbook* can also be used independently by individuals or couples.

▸▸ **ROPP VIDEO:** downloadable vidcasts containing Bible teaching from Dr. Walker Moore. These vidcasts, matched to each session of the *Rite of Passage Parenting Workbook*, support and supplement the ROPP principles.

▸▸ **ROPP DOWNLOADS:** visuals, diagrams, Facilitators' Helps, and additional Fix-It forms for the *Rite of Passage Parenting Workbook* along with a PowerPoint presentation for teaching the ROPP basics.

▸▸ **ROPP DEVOTIONS:** weekly devotions written to encourage you as a Rite of Passage Parent.

▸▸ **ROPP EVENTS:** link to opportunities specifically designed to provide your child with a rite of passage event, available through Awe Star Ministries.

▸▸ **ROPP TALK:** opportunities to interact with other Rite of Passage Parents.

▸▸ **ROPP REVIEW:** space for your personal assessment of the book and/or workbook.

▸▸ **ROPP CONTACT INFORMATION:** schedule and contact information for the teaching ministry of Walker Moore; ways to have Walker or another ROPP/Awe Star representative speak to your church or organization.